I HAVE A SUPPLY

by

Nancy Dufresne

BOOKS BY DR. ED DUFRESNE

Praying God's Word

Devil, Don't Touch My Stuff!

There's A Healer In The House

Faithfulness: The Road to Divine Promotion

The Footsteps Of A Prophet

Golden Nuggets For Longevity

Things That Pertain To The Spirit

How To Be Rich God's Way

BOOKS BY NANCY DUFRESNE

Daily Healing Bread From God's Table

His Presence Shall Be My Dwelling Place

Victory In The Name

There Came A Sound From Heaven:
The Life Story of Dr. Ed Dufresne

The Healer Divine

Visitations From God

Responding To The Holy Spirit

God: The Revealer Of Secrets

A Supernatural Prayer Life

Causes

TABLE OF CONTENTS

PART III - PROSPERITY TRUTHS

INTRODUCTION

Proverbs 10:22, KJV
The blessing of the Lord, it maketh rich, and he addeth no sorrow with it.

Proverbs 10:22, Amplified
The blessing of the Lord – it makes [truly] rich, and He adds no sorrow with it [neither does toiling increase it].

The word "rich" means a full supply. A man who lives under the blessing of the Lord will be fully supplied, and every arena of his life will prosper: his spiritual life, his marriage, family, health, relationships, business and finances. True prosperity that comes from the Lord affects every arena.

When God prospers you, He does not steal from one arena of your life to increase another arena. God will not steal from your spiritual life to increase your business life. He will not steal from your church life and serving in your local church to increase you on the job and in the work place. He will not steal from your family life to increase your income. When God blesses you, every arena of life receives of that increase.

Being in God's will, growing in the knowledge of God, and releasing your faith in God's blessing on your life enables the blessing of the Lord to flow unhindered. Increasing work hours will not increase this blessing, but obedience to live out God's plan and being faithful to that plan will.

Obedience to God's plan carries its own provision with it. Proverbs 28:20, "*A faithful man shall ABOUND with blessings....*" Faithfulness will cause blessings to abound in your life. God has not left us to live by the sweat of the brow, toiling in our own human effort, limited to our own natural talents, abilities and education.

We have the blessing of God on our lives, and that blessing can bring us into a place that no human effort could carry us to.

Many spend their whole lives trying to protect their money because money gained by human effort has sorrow attached to it. But those who live under the blessing of the Lord are to protect the blessing of God on them, for, "*The blessing of the Lord, it maketh rich, and he addeth no sorrow with it*" (Proverbs 10:22).

God's blessing reaches beyond your finances and makes you rich in every arena of life. Go ahead, live as rich as you are!

PART I
MY GOD SHALL SUPPLY

CHAPTER 1

The Cure for Lack

As born again children of God, we never have to be worried or occupied with the things that trouble the world. John 8:36 tells us, *"If the Son therefore shall make you free, ye shall be free indeed."* Because Jesus has set us free, we are to live free from the fear of sickness, failure, lack, and anything else that would strike terror in the hearts of unsaved men. Let us live as free as we are!

One of the foremost fears that plagues the world is the fear of lack. But Jesus stood up in the synagogue of His hometown in Nazareth and announced to mankind, *"The Spirit of the Lord is upon me, because he hath anointed me to PREACH THE GOSPEL TO THE POOR; he hath sent me to heal the brokenhearted, to preach deliverance to the captives, and recovering of sight to the blind, to set at liberty them that are bruised. To preach the acceptable Year of the Lord"* (Luke 4:18 & 19). Notice the first thing Jesus proclaims that He came to do in this passage of His job description, *"...He hath anointed me to preach the gospel to the poor...."* Jesus shows us that the Gospel is for the poor. The Gospel is the cure for poverty. The Gospel is the cure for lack.

In the financial arena, the Gospel is the cure for lack. Many who are in financial difficulty think that money is their cure for lack, and that their need is more money; but according to the Word, their need is more Gospel. Money, paychecks, jobs and income have never been the cure for lack, for if these things run out or come to an end, they would be right back in lack. Money, jobs and incomes are avenues through which God meets our needs, but they are not our source; they are not our provider – God is!

Proverbs 10:22 tells us, "*The blessing of the Lord, it maketh rich, and he addeth no sorrow with it.*" It's the blessing of the Lord that makes us rich, not our money or income.

There are many people in the earth who have millions of dollars, but they're not rich; their lives are full of lack in other arenas. Not only that, you can have millions of dollars but still be broke because of the way you think.

Our jobs and professions are avenues that God uses to meet our financial needs, but they are not our source and provider; God is, and the Gospel is how God makes known to us how large and deep is His supply and provision for our lives.

When believers fall behind financially, the first step to take is to increase their intake of the Word. Since the Gospel is the cure for lack, you have to increase feeding, meditating and acting on the Word to experience increase of finances.

The Word tells us in Third John 1:2, "*Beloved, I wish above all things that thou mayest prosper and be in health, even as thy soul prospereth.*" John was writing this letter as he was moved on by the Holy Ghost, so we could rightly say that the Holy Ghost said, "*Beloved, I wish above all things that thou mayest prosper....*" Did you know that the desire for your prosperity originated with God, and not with you? As much as it is your own desire to prosper, God desires prosperity for you more than you desire it for yourself.

Psalms 35:27 tells us, "*Let them shout for joy, and be glad, that favour my righteous cause: yea, let them say continually, Let the Lord be magnified, WHICH HATH PLEASURE IN THE PROSPERITY OF HIS SERVANT.*" Your prosperity is God's pleasure. It pleases Him when you prosper. It doesn't offend Him, it pleases Him.

Religion has taught people that money is unholy. The love of money is the root of all evil (First Timothy 6:10), but money isn't evil. Money takes on the character of the one who possesses it. If a man is evil, he uses money for evil purposes, but if a man is righteous, he uses money for righteous purposes. It pleases God when His children prosper, for then the money they possess will be used for the righteous cause of establishing His covenant on the earth, and not for evil causes.

God wants all your needs fully supplied, and it pleases Him when you have more than enough. Psalms 35:27 says, "...*Let the Lord be magnified, which hath pleasure in the prosperity of his SERVANT.*" Under the Old Testament, they were God's servants, but under the New Testament, we are His sons. Now, if God took pleasure in the prosperity of His servants, how much more He would take pleasure in the prosperity of His sons. Religion tells people that God is only interested in our spiritual lives, but that's not true. God is interested in every single arena of our lives.

As a parent, I am interested first and foremost in the spiritual welfare of our children, but I'm not only interested in their spiritual lives. I'm interested in every arena of their lives. It matters to me that our children have the food and clothes they need. It matters to me that they have the cars and the homes they need. It matters to me that they have money to pay their bills and money to spend on the things they desire to have. Well, if I'm interested that our children have the things they need and want for their everyday lives, how much more God is interested that His children have all they need and want for their everyday lives.

It pleases God when we prosper and have all we need in this life. For when we prosper, He knows that His work on the earth will be funded.

As we prosper, we are warned, "*But thou shalt remember the Lord thy God: for it is he that giveth the power to get* (produce) *wealth that he may establish his covenant....*" We must remember why God has blessed us, so we can fund His work in the earth. As we put His work in the earth first and fund it, then we will be funded, and all our needs will be met.

As I stated previously, if you fall behind financially, the Word is the cure; increase your intake and acting on the Word. Many think that their need is more money, so they may get an additional job or work longer hours. That is fine if that is how God directs you, but don't leave out increasing your intake of the Word, for that's the sure cure!

Most of the time, when Christians increase their work hours, it pulls them away from devotional time with the Lord. It pulls them away from their church attendance and serving in their local church, but when the Lord blesses you, He adds no sorrow with it. When God blesses you, every arena of your life increases. When God increases you financially, He won't have to steal from your family and home life, from your church or from serving in your local church. There's no sorrow with His blessing, no subtraction from other arenas with His blessing, only increase.

Your job and income isn't your provider, God is. Your job and profession are simply avenues through which God blesses you, but don't limit God to only those avenues. If you think God can only supply for you through your job, then you'll limit Him. God blesses what we set our hands to, but don't limit what you can set your hand to.

Divine Ideas

I was talking to a dear friend of mine who had served as an administrator for world-wide ministries over the past 60 years. As a businessman, he had made his first million dollars when he was in his early 20's, but God opened doors for him to be an administrator for different ministries.

As an administrator, he recognized that these ministries couldn't pay him the kind of income he had when he worked in the business world, but he wasn't willing to miss God and give up working in the ministry just so he could have a larger salary from the business world. As he brought his supply to these ministers and ministries, God continued to increase him.

One day, he told me, "I've never prayed and asked God for money. I've always prayed and asked God for divine ideas. I knew that if God gave me a divine idea, the money would come with the idea."

But you have to understand that he was using the gifts God gave him to further the Gospel. He wasn't just using his gifts in the pursuit of money.

God gave him many divine ideas. The ideas God gave him took very little of his time, so he could devote himself to the ministries God had assigned him to. He understood that the Gospel was his supply, not money. That's why he prayed for divine ideas. He didn't pursue money; he pursued God's plan, for he knew the divine supply was with God's divine plan.

Those who think money is their answer will pursue money, but the pursuit of money is a vain pursuit that carries much sorrow with it. Pursue God's plan for your life, give the Word its proper attention, and let God's increase supply your need.

Christians need to believe God for divine ideas that will help fund the Gospel and their own lives.

One Woman's Divine Idea

I tell the story of a single mom who received a divine idea from God. She was attending a service of an evangelist who came to minister in her local church. At the end of the service, while an offering was being received for the evangelist, the Spirit of God spoke to her telling her to give $1000 to his ministry.

For a moment, she argued with the Lord. "Lord, I'm a single mom. I don't even have a $1000, and that's a lot of money for me." But she knew God wanted her to do it, so she wrote on an offering envelope that she was committing to send the evangelist $1000 within thirty days.

God wasn't trying to press her into financial hard ship; He was trying to press her past financial hardship.

That night she went home and prayed, "I don't have $1000 to give, but I believe for You to provide me with it."

As she was praying, the Lord reminded her how she had decorated some barrettes and given them as gifts to some of her family and friends for Christmas, and how much everyone had loved them. She had the idea to make some of those barrettes and ask if she could sell them in a boutique her friend owned.

She contacted her friend and asked if it would be okay with her if she set up a table in her boutique on the following Saturday and sell the barrettes. Her friend kindly agreed, so she spent the rest of the week making the barrettes.

The following Saturday she was in the boutique with her table set up displaying the many barrette designs she had made. After a while, a woman walked into the boutique and walked around, finally making her way over to the table this single mom had set up. The woman seemed entirely engrossed as she picked up each barrette one by one, examining them carefully. After several minutes the woman asked the single mom:

"Did you make these?"

"Yes I did," was her reply.

"I'll take 50,000 of them!"

The woman was a buyer of a nationwide, high-end department store. Not only did this single mom have her $1000 to pay off her commitment, but she had a source of income.

God has divine ideas that faith can lay hold of. The divine idea for this single mom sounded like an "everyday" idea. It really didn't sound very spectacular or divine, but it was, for God had given it to her.

Don't miss a divine idea by thinking that it doesn't sound very spectacular. Remember what Third John 1:2 says, "*Beloved, I wish above all things that thou mayest PROSPER and be in health, EVEN AS THY SOUL PROSPERTH.*"

Some may ask, "Well, if God desires for me to prosper, then why am I not prospering?" John tells us in this verse that our prosperity is connected to our soul (the soul is made up of the mind, the will and the emotions). In other words, you will prosper to the level that your soul prospers, and your soul prospers as you renew your mind with the Word.

To renew your mind, you must feed, meditate and act on God's Word. When you know what God says about your prosperity, and you think in line with God's Word, then His Word will make a difference in your finances.

Remember what I stated earlier. The word is the cure for lack, not money. John is saying the same thing to us in Third John 1:2 when he tells us that we will prosper as our soul prospers. The only way to have your soul prosper is to feed and act on God's Word. Those who think that more money is the answer to their financial situation will often neglect their real answer, which is more revelation of the Word of God.

If you find yourself in a difficult place financially, set extra time aside to feed on His Word and to wait before God in prayer. As you do, wisdom and light will come to you. Then as you obey what He says, you will move into increase.

CHAPTER 2

Jesus Was Made Poor, We Are Made Rich

II Corinthians 8:9
For ye know the grace of our Lord Jesus Christ, that, though he was rich, yet for your sakes, he became poor, that ye through his poverty might be rich.

Religion has wrongly taught that this scripture means that Jesus was made poor spiritually so that you could be rich spiritually. But to be spiritually poor, Jesus would have had to have been out of fellowship with His Father. Jesus was never out of fellowship with the Father, so this scripture wasn't referring to Jesus becoming spiritually poor. This passage is referring to financial poverty. He was made poor, so we could take His place in being rich. "...he became poor, that ye through his poverty might become rich."

What does it mean to be rich? To be rich doesn't necessarily mean that you'll be a millionaire, but it means that you will have a full supply.

When we look at Jesus during the span of His earthly ministry, when did we ever see Him poor? If Jesus had a need, we always saw that need fully supplied.

When Jesus wanted to feed the multitude who had been with Him for several days, He didn't have the resources to do that, but He had God's plan of how to do it. He had the disciples bring Him the little boy's lunch which contained five loaves and two fishes. Jesus took the bread and fish, "...*and looking up to heaven, he BLESSED, and brake, and gave the loaves to his disciples, and the disciples to the multitude*" (Matthew 14:19). Jesus didn't curse the five loaves and two fishes by saying, "This isn't enough." Rather, He blessed it. When he blessed it, what wasn't enough became more than enough.

If you don't have enough, don't curse it by complaining. It's our job to bless what we do have, and when we do, God will make it become more than enough.

In another instance, when Jesus needed the money to pay taxes, He told Peter to go fishing. Jesus knew that the first fish that came to the hook would have the necessary money in its mouth, and it did!

Jesus always received the supply He needed. He was never poor during His earthly ministry for the supply always came to Him.

Even at Jesus' crucifixion, the soldiers recognized the great value of the coat He wore. These soldiers were used to stripping the valuables from their defeated enemies to keep for themselves, but even these soldiers, who had little regard for the property of their enemies, didn't want to damage this coat that is described as being seamless. For it to be seamless, it was woven with one continuous thread. This was not the wardrobe of a poor man. It was the coat of a man of wealth.

Since we never saw Jesus poor during His earthly ministry, then when did He become poor that we might be made rich?

He became poor at the same place He became sin, at Calvary.

As He took our place in sin, He also took our place in sickness, and He took our place in poverty. The sin of mankind was laid upon Him, and He bore the penalty. The sickness and disease of suffering humanity was laid upon Him, and He took it away from us. Likewise, the curse of poverty was laid upon Him so that we might be made rich. He did all this at Calvary.

We can't be saved by works we've done. How are we saved? We are saved by faith. We can't be healed by works we've done. How are we healed? We are healed by faith. Likewise, we are not made rich by works we've done. How are we made rich? We are made rich by faith. All Christ did for us at Calvary is received one way, by faith. We can't earn it. Salvation, healing and prosperity are free gifts to those who will receive it.

Because you're born again, healing belongs to you. You don't have to try to get healed. It's yours because you were born into it. Likewise, you don't have to try to become rich. When you were born again, you were born into prosperity.

When I was born, I was born in America, so I am an American citizen. I never get out of bed thinking, "I've got to try to be an American today." No, I'm an American because I was born an American. I don't have to try to be an American. I am an American. I don't have to try to become what I am. You can't separate me from being an American; that's what I am. It's my inheritance.

Likewise, I don't have to try to be rich. I am made rich because I was born into it when I was born again. He was made poor so that I could be made rich. It is my inheritance.

This is one of the truths of God's Word that believers must renew their minds with. Many Christians don't have a revelation of how rich they are because of what Jesus did for them, so they are trying to get rich. But those with a renewed mind see that at the time we were born again, we were born into the prosperity He has provided for all His children.

Talk about how Jesus was made poor so that we could be made rich. Our job is to meditate on this and confess it continually. As we do, it will become real to us. If faced with financial difficulty, we must continue to hold fast to our confession of this in the face of every contrary circumstance.

Meditate on the following truths. Say them over and over to yourself until they become real to you. Because Jesus took my place in poverty, He has given me His wealth. I am rich because I'm a child of God. I was born into this wealth when I was born again. It is part of my inheritance. I'm not trying to be rich, I am rich. You can't separate me from being rich; that's what I am because of what Jesus did for me. It's not money that makes me rich; it's what Jesus did for me that makes me rich. Because I am rich, all the money I need comes to me. All the divine ideas I need come to me from God. All the doors I need opened open up to me. The blessing of the Lord makes me rich, and He adds no sorrow with it.

This is what you must renew your mind with. You must continually and daily confess these things to be true in your life. As you build this into your spirit and your mind, your days of struggle will be over, and you'll begin to live as rich as you are.

CHAPTER 3

The Supply is for the Need

Philippians 4:19
But my God shall supply all your needs according to his riches in glory by Christ Jesus.

Just by living on the earth, we're going to face needs, but the Word lets us know that no matter what needs we may face, God shall supply all our needs.

"Lack" and "need" are not the same thing. If you have a need, that doesn't mean you are in lack. "Lack" means that there is not a supply. But God lets us know that every need His children will ever face has a supply, so we lack for nothing.

The unsaved man has lack because he can't be assured of a supply for the things he will face in life. The Christian will never again face lack, for God has provided a supply for every need His children will face. Jesus took our place in "lack" at Calvary so that we would never be in "lack" again. He paid the price to bring us into "supply". That's what Paul reveals to us when he wrote in Philippians 4:19, *"But my God shall supply all your needs according to his riches in glory BY CHRIST JESUS."*

By what Jesus did for us, He brought us out of "lack" and delivered us into "supply". You will never face lack again for the supply of God is yours, and it's an unlimited supply. There's no bottom to His supply. It's an endless supply that is inexhaustible.

Satan seeks to accuse us by telling us that if we had faith, we wouldn't have a need, but that's not true, for God will lead us to create a need so that we can qualify for the supply. When Paul wrote, "*But my God shall SUPPLY all your NEEDS....*" God is letting us know that the supply is for the need.

You must have a "need" to qualify for the "supply". To have a need is not a negative because there is a supply for the need. The supply of God is for every spiritual, mental, physical, and material need. God isn't just interested in your spiritual needs, but He's interested in any need in every arena of your life. God is so interested in the needs of His children that He did something about those needs, He provided a supply for all of them.

When we are faced with a need, we aren't to be overwhelmed and worried about it, for we have a supply for it. We must have a need to qualify for the supply.

Did you know that God will lead you to create a need? Why? He will lead you to create a need because He has a supply for the need. So, He will lead you to create a need, so He can bring the supply to you that He has for your life.

"That's Our House!"

When we moved from Tulsa, Oklahoma to California in 1991, we rented a home for a couple of years. After renting a home for two years, one day Ed handed me a local real estate magazine with a beautiful house on the cover. When he handed me the magazine, he said, "That's our house! When I walked into the store this morning, this magazine was lying on a rack. When I saw it, God told me that it was our house."

I knew that when my husband heard from God, that God would bring it to pass, but my mind wanted to start calculating the finances immediately. I'm the one that handled the paying of the bills, and I knew that in the natural there was no way we could afford a home. But I also knew to turn off my mind because the mind can't calculate the supply of God! God was leading us to create a bigger need because He had a bigger supply for us.

If you try to mentally calculate how God is going to supply the need He leads you to create, you could miss your supply. Reason is doubt in disguise. Your mind can't "figure out" all that God can supply. Just know that if He leads you to create a need, it's because He has a supply He wants to bring into your life.

Create a Need

Remember the story I told in a previous chapter about the single mom who received a divine idea from God? God led her to create barrettes, and then a buyer for a nationwide department store bought 50,000 of them.

How did that all start? God led the single mom to create a need. He told her to pledge to give a thousand dollars to a traveling minister who came to her church. God was not trying to press her into financial hardship. He was trying to press her past financial hardship. He had a supply for her, but she didn't qualify for the supply until she created the need. He had to get her to create the need, so He could bring her the supply. If this single mom would have let mental calculations keep her from making that thousand dollar pledge to the traveling minister, she would have never exercised her faith for the supply, and she would have never received the divine idea or the supply.

Follow the Spirit

One of the keys to flowing in the supply of God is to learn to follow the Spirit of God. In one vision of Jesus that Kenneth E. Hagin had, Jesus told him, "If you'll learn to follow My Spirit, I'll make you rich. I'm not opposed to My people being rich. I'm opposed to them being covetous."

"Rich" doesn't mean that God's going to make all his children millionaires. "Rich" means to have "a full supply." God wants all of his children to have a full supply. That means that you would have enough for all your personal needs with plenty left over so you can be a generous giver.

Genesis 13 tells us that Abraham was very rich, but in the chapter before that, God told Abraham, "...*and I will bless thee... and thou shalt BE A BLESSING*" (Genesis 12:2). When God blessed Abraham, He didn't just have Abraham in mind, but He had those in mind that Abraham would bless. God never intends that any of us be blessed just so we can consume it all on ourselves, but God wants us to be mindful to be a blessing. How can that happen? It can only happen if we are fully supplied. He wants you to be rich to have enough for all your needs and to have more than enough, so you can be a blessing to others.

Jesus told Brother Hagin, "If you'll learn to follow My Spirit, I'll make you rich." Following the Spirit is a vital key to living in the supply of God.

The Spirit of God told Ed that the house on the cover of the real estate magazine was ours. Because we didn't have the finances in the natural to purchase a house, we were only assured of the supply as long as it was the Spirit who led us to purchase the home.

Ed had a real estate agent show us the house, and we were sure it was the plan of God. Although our heads could not figure out how God would financially supply it, we had peace in our hearts about it.

Isaiah 55:12 tells us, "*For ye shall go out with joy, AND BE LED FORTH WITH PEACE....*" When the Spirit is leading in a particular direction, there will always be peace in your spirit, even if the mind is giving you trouble. The Amplified Bible of Colossians 3:15 instructs us, "*And let the peace...from Christ rule (act as umpire continually) in your hearts [deciding and settling with finality all questions that arise in your minds....*" In a game, the umpire makes the call, and if there is a dispute about the call, the umpire's call stands. The Word is telling us that if there is a dispute about what direction to go or what decision to make, let peace make the call. Follow peace, and you'll always go the right direction.

We followed the peace in our hearts, and we pursued the purchase of the home. The home had been built two years earlier, but had sat empty. It was owned out right by an older woman who lived in Los Angeles, California, but her two sons were handling her properties. After viewing the house, Ed met with the two brothers to discuss the purchase of the home. After the meeting, they went to their mother and told her that a preacher was interested in buying the home.

Since she was a Christian woman, she asked, "What's the preacher's name?"

"His name is Ed Dufresne," her sons told her.

She exclaimed, "Fifteen years ago I was healed in one of his services! You do whatever you need to do to get him in that house!" And they did.

When Ed saw that home on the magazine cover, he had no way of knowing how God would move to supply us with that house, but God had a plan. Until we created the need, we never would have moved into the supply. God had a supply for us, but we could only receive it if we followed the Spirit in creating the need.

Moving Forward into Supply

God will lead you to create a need. We see accounts all throughout the Bible where God led His people to create needs. One such account was when He delivered His people out of Egypt. On their way to the Promised Land, God led them to the Red Sea, but even as they followed God's guidance, they came to a place where they were hemmed in – mountains to the left, mountains to the right, the Red Sea in front of them, and an angry Egyptian army whose firstborn were dead. It looked like there was no way out for the Hebrews, but God had a supply for them although it wasn't very apparent at first.

Psalms 77:19 & 20 (Amplified Bible) reads, "*Your way [in delivering Your people] was through the sea, and Your paths through the great waters, yet Your footsteps were not traceable, but were obliterated. You led Your people like a flock by the hand of Moses and Aaron.*" These verses show us that God had supplied a route of escape for His people. Before they had ever reached the Red Sea, God had already walked through the Red Sea making footprints for His people to follow. The waters hid His footprints, but at Moses' command, the waters parted and revealed the path God's footprints had made. He had a supply for His people although not immediately visible. However, as they followed His leading, the supply of His path became visible. The supply of a parted sea didn't show up until their toes were at the water's edge. The waters didn't part for them while they were in Egypt. The waters didn't part when they reached the sea.

Let's see what God said to them. "*And the Lord said unto Moses, Wherefore criest thou unto me? Speak unto the children of Israel, that they GO FORWARD: But lift thou up thy rod, and stretch out thine hand over the sea, and divide it: and the children of Israel shall go on dry ground through the midst of the sea*" (Exodus 14:15 & 16). It wasn't until they moved forward in faith, and Moses stretched out the rod that the supply of the parted Red Sea appeared. Even though they were at the place where God led them, the Red Sea wouldn't have parted if they hadn't acted in faith on what God said.

You can be at the place God led you to be, but you still must exercise faith if you are to receive the supply that belongs to you. It won't just come automatically; you must exercise your faith to receive it. Many times the supply won't show up a month in advance, a week in advance, or even a day in advance, but do as God told the Hebrews, and go forward. The supply will show up just as your toes reach the edge of the water, the edge of your need. Don't worry, for God has a supply for your need, and it's faith that receives the supply that belongs to the need.

It Will Be There When You Need It

Years ago, I read the life story of Corrie ten Boom, who lived in Holland and helped hide Jews during the Holocaust. Her family all lived together as they created a place of safety for Jews fleeing imprisonment in concentration camps.

One day, Corrie ten Boom voiced her concern to her elderly father, "If we were ever caught for hiding Jews, I don't know if I would have enough strength to face imprisonment and possible death."

"Corrie," her father answered, "do you remember the times when you were a little girl and we would travel by train? I would purchase the tickets months in advance, but I didn't give you your ticket then. I didn't even give it to you when we arrived at the train station. I would hand it to you right before the porter asked for it. You didn't need the ticket until the porter came. When the time comes for you to face any test, God will supply the strength."

Even so, the supply for every need we face will show up on time. No, the supply might not show up a month in advance, or even a week in advance, but when you need it, it will be there if you will hold fast to God's Word. The flesh would like to have the supply in hand well before the supply is needed, but faith will rest before the supply shows up, for it knows that when the need shows up, the supply will show up on time.

Paul tells us, *"But my God shall supply ALL your needs...."* You will never face a need that doesn't have a supply. Every need has a supply, and its faith that receives it. It doesn't just come to you automatically because it belongs to you; you must release your faith daily for it.

An Easy Flowing Supply

During the Great Depression of the 1930's, work, money and food was scarce for many of this nation. Many of those who grew up during the depression faced great hardship and struggle that left its mark on them. Money was so hard to come by during those years for millions of people that it shaped the way they thought about and handled money. As they had children, they passed that hardship toward supply down to their own children, so the depression marked several generations.

The supply God has for His children is not a hard supply, but an easy supply. We don't have to coerce it out of the hand of God. He has already made provision for our every need, for He longs for our prosperity.

Just as the depression left its negative mark on people's thinking, we need to allow God's supply to leave its positive mark on how Christians think. We need to know that God has a supply for us, and it's an easy flowing supply, not hard.

Yes, the enemy seeks to hinder the flow of God's supply into our lives, but as we exercise our authority over him, our supply will reach our lives. Because God blesses us through the hands of men, the enemy will try to interfere and hinder men's obedience to God. But if the supply is slow in coming, never accuse God of withholding or slowing down the supply, for He has already made provision for all we will ever need, and He has freely provided it for us. If the supply is slow in coming, know that it is the enemy's doings and not God's. It is the enemy's strategy to seek to interfere, hinder and slow down the supply so that you will doubt God's Word to be true. But if you will hold fast to God's Word and not waver in the face of circumstances, your faith will propel God's easy flowing supply past any of the enemy's obstacles and hindrances, and it will reach your need.

3 Steps to Receiving Supply

When it comes to receiving financial supply, there are three steps that you must take to receive the supply God has provided for you:

1) Claim how much money you need.

2) Tell Satan to take his hands off your money.

3) Tell the angels that are assigned to your life to go and cause the money to come. Angels are sent to assist us; they are ministering spirits sent forth to minister for us. They know how to influence people and situations so that supply will flow to you. God's Word tells us that angels hearken to the Word of God, so as we speak God's Word, they move to cooperate with it.

The supply that God has provided for our lives is already on the earth. We are not trying to get God to send our supply down from heaven; it's already on the earth.

In Genesis 1 we see God create the heavens and the earth. When he created the earth, He supplied it with everything man would ever need. After creation was complete, then He created man. Man was the purpose for the creation of the earth. The earth was created to provide a suitable habitation for man and for all man would ever need. The earth is to serve man and his needs. God had man's supply in mind when He created the earth. God fully supplied the earth before He placed man here. By doing this, He shows us that He provided the supply before man ever faced a need. We must always remember that every need we face already has a supply. We must just release our faith to receive that supply, and allow the supply to annihilate the need.

We are to allow what God tells us in Philippians 4:19 to renew our thinking, "*But my God shall supply all your need according to his riches in glory by Christ Jesus.*" The emphasis in the minds of many believers is how great their needs are, but God wants this verse to give us His emphasis, which is how great God's supply for our lives is. No longer are we to be need conscious, but we are to be supply conscious. The supply was provided before there was ever a need.

When God leads us to create a need, our first thought is no longer to be occupied with the awareness of the need, but we are to train ourselves to be more aware of the supply that is ours. We are not to be need conscious, but we are to be mindful of the God who supplies. Don't talk about the need, but talk about the God who supplies your need.

CHAPTER 4

Don't Linger in the Need

Difficulties can arise in our lives when we linger in a need instead of pass through a place of need.

When God delivered the Hebrews out of Egypt, He led them through the Red Sea and into the wilderness. The journey through the wilderness should have only taken a matter of days, but because they refused to exercise faith while in the wilderness, they lingered in a place that God only intended for them to pass through. God led them to that wilderness, but He didn't intend for them to linger there, but unbelief held them there.

There are places of need we face in life that we should just pass through, but if we don't exercise our faith when we face that need, we will linger in a place of need too long. In referring to the Hebrews lingering in the wilderness for 40 years, Hebrews 4:2 tells us, "*For unto us was the gospel preached , as well as unto them: but the word preached did not profit them, NOT BEING MIXED WITH FAITH IN THEM THAT HEARD IT.*" Notice that the Word didn't profit them. Why? It did not profit them because they didn't mix faith with the Word that was preached to them.

The Word of God is the help and the answer in the face of every need, but if faith isn't mixed with that Word, you won't profit from it. When faith is added to the Word, it works, but without your faith mixed in with the Word, it won't work for you; it won't profit you.

How do you mix faith with the Word? Your tongue is the mixer that mixes your faith in with God's Word. You don't get in life what you believe; it's not enough to believe. Jesus said in Mark 11:23 "*...he shall have whatsoever he SAITH.*" Jesus didn't say that you'll have what you believe, but He did say that you'll have what you say. The Bible tells us that the demons believe and tremble; it's not just believing that receives from God, but you must say what you believe to activate your faith.

Romans 10:17 tells us, "*So faith COMETH by hearing, and hearing by the Word of God.*" This verse tells us how faith comes, by hearing God's Word. Although faith comes by hearing, faith doesn't operate by hearing. How does faith operate, or how is faith released? By speaking, speaking what God's Word says.

Yes, you must believe, but you must also speak. Romans 10:10 says, "*For with the heart man believeth into righteousness; and with the MOUTH confession is made unto salvation.*" God is letting us know that faith must be in two places, in your heart and in your mouth. When you hear the Word, you believe. When you speak the Word, you receive.

The supply God has provided for your life won't flow automatically. You must mix your faith in with the Word. How do you do that? Your tongue is the mixer, mixing your faith and the Word together. When you mix your words of faith with God's Word, then the Word starts moving and annihilating the need with God's supply.

I can remember one time in particular when our church finances lingered too long in a place of need. I started praying about our situation, and God began teaching me some of these truths. He showed me where I had missed it. He taught me that when you're faced with a need, it is right to rest in God, but you still must be aggressive toward the need. Even when resting in God, we must still express our faith in God's supply that eliminates the need. Resting in God doesn't dismiss us from expressing and releasing our faith. It takes real effort to diligently exercise our faith in God's supply when we are faced with a need. Just because you may be good at not worrying doesn't mean you're good at expressing your faith.

So, I got our staff together and we began to actively and diligently release our faith daily in God's supply to annihilate the need. I gave the staff a list of scriptures that showed how God has provided a supply for our need, and I made a list of the needs that we needed supplied. Every day we called out those scriptures to God and released our faith, claiming that God's power was working in our situation. We also called out each need and spoke that the supply was coming to everyone of our needs. As we diligently did this on a daily basis, we quickly saw a turn-around of the situation. But just because we saw increase, we didn't stop releasing our faith. We continued to meet daily to mix our faith with God's Word. It just took us a few minutes each day, but as soon as we diligently spoke our faith regarding our situation, supply immediately began moving to annihilate the need.

We don't want to linger in a need, so we are to diligently mix our faith in with God's Word and move into the supply.

Your Supply is Waiting on You

You may have needs to show up that catch you by surprise, but your needs didn't catch God by surprise. He's already provided for your need before the need was even created. God doesn't just start preparing a supply for you at the time the need appears. He provided your supply long ago. Hebrews 4:3, The Amplified Bible, tells us, "... *[His] works had been COMPLETED and PREPARED [and WAITING FOR ALL WHO WOULD BELIEVE] from the foundation of the world.*" God is letting us know that He completed and prepared the supply for every need you'll face in life at the same time He founded the world.

Hebrews 4:3 tells us that all that God has completed and prepared for us is, "*...waiting for all who would believe....*" God's supply for your life is waiting for your faith. So, start releasing your faith in God's supply by calling the supply to come into your life. It is waiting for you!

Faith is for the Need

The devil may try to accuse you by saying that if you have a need, it's because your faith isn't working. But remember what I stated earlier, that having a need is not a negative. Just by being alive, needs are going to arise, so don't let the devil accuse you of not having faith just because a need arises. To have a need is not a negative.

Jesus faced needs time and time again throughout His earthly ministry, but we never saw Him in lack, for He always received the supply for every need He faced.

Just because you face needs doesn't mean that you lack faith. Paul stated in Philippians 4:12, the Amplified Bible, "*I know how to be abased and live humbly in straitened circumstances, and I know also how to enjoy plenty and live in abundance....*" To read this shows us that this apostle of God faced needs. He faced them knowing that God had already provided a supply for every need he would face. He didn't see a need as a negative, for he knew he had a supply and exercised his faith in God's supply for his life. Bring your faith in God's supply to every need, and no need will be a negative in your life.

Count it All Joy

When we understand how far-reaching God's supply for our life is, then we can do what James instructs us to do in James 1:2. "*My brethren, COUNT IT ALL JOY when ye fall into diverse temptations.*" The test and trial isn't a joy, but we are to count it a joy because although God isn't the One who sent the test, He provided the supply for every test we will face. We count it a joy for the opportunity to stand on God's Word, express our faith, and receive our supply.

We are to rejoice in the face of need because we trust in the God who supplies all our needs. In fact, until you begin to rejoice, you won't come out of that place of need. Isaiah 55:12 tells us, "*For ye shall GO OUT WITH JOY, and be led forth with peace....*" The exit door out of every test is joy. When you believe that God has your supply in the face of your need, then you can rejoice.

There's only one reason why you wouldn't rejoice, and that is if you don't believe that there is a supply for every need. But we choose to believe that God supplies all our needs. Since we believe this, then we can rejoice.

CHAPTER 5

Following the Spirit

There are some supplies God has for you that you'll never receive until you follow the leading of the Spirit in creating the need. Many perceive the Spirit leading them to do something, but because they see what a place of need it will put them in, they fail to follow the Spirit. They don't want to go to that place of need. But never be afraid to follow the Spirit in creating a need; God's supply awaits you there!

My husband tells of the time he was with Dr. Lester Sumrall in a crusade. After one of the services, Dr. Sumrall invited Ed into his hotel room. "I need you to go with me to my hotel room and act as a witness to the signing of a contract."

Ed followed him into the room as Dr. Sumrall pulled a contract out of his briefcase and laid it on the desk. He signed his name to the contract then passed it to Ed to sign as a witness. After they had signed, Dr. Sumrall asked Ed, "Do you know what I just signed? It's a contract to purchase another television station for five million dollars. I don't have five million dollars, but God told me to do it!"

Ed was getting a lesson in faith! By signing that contract, Dr. Sumrall was led by the Spirit to put himself in a place of need. Dr. Sumrall was fully aware of the position of need that contract put him in, but he was more aware that God had a supply for that place of need. If Dr. Sumrall would have never had enough faith to follow God into a place of need, he would not have been in the place to receive God's supply of five million dollars.

To have faith enough to receive the supply, you have to have faith enough to create the need; you have to have faith enough to follow the Spirit into a place of need.

You can't mentally figure out and calculate how the supply will come and where it will come from, but you are to still have faith enough to create the need God leads you to create. If you try to believe God with your mind, you'll never create the need God leads you to create. You can't believe God with your mind. If you try to, you'll fail. You'll find yourself swimming in a sea of reasoning and questions, and you'll end up on the shore of doubt and unbelief. To follow God's Spirit in creating a need, you have to turn off and ignore the mind and believe with your heart.

God's Plan Requires God's Supply

Years ago, God spoke to my heart saying, "I have another house for you," but it wasn't until about five years later that we found that house. In fact, we weren't actively looking for a house, but it began stirring in my Spirit that we would soon move into a new home. We were visiting someone when they told us about a house that had just been built and would soon be on the market. So, we went and walked through the house. When we were walking through it, it seemed to me that this was the house God had told me about five years earlier.

That night I began to pray about that house. I asked God, "Is this the house you have for us?" I didn't want to assume it was, for I didn't want to settle for that house if He had something even better for us. That's where a lot of people miss it. They settle on something without talking to God about it first, and they end up settling for less than God had for them. God spoke to me saying, "That's the house I have for you."

Now, remember what I wrote earlier, you may or may not hear God's voice. Don't seek to hear a voice, but do seek to get direction clear in your spirit before you make a move.

When God told us that the home was ours, there was no way in the natural that we could afford that home. I've noticed something about God. He never consults with your checkbook to see if you have enough money to accomplish what He tells you to do. He has prepared a supply for everything He's called you to do, for your checkbook and your paycheck could never supply all that he has called you to accomplish. His call and His assignments for your life require His supply. You can't fulfill God's plan for your life without God's supply!

When God told us that was our house, we knew that it was going to require God's supply to get us into that home, but we also knew that until we created the need, we didn't qualify for the supply! When you know the Spirit is leading you to create the need, then you know that there's a supply He wants to move into your life.

God worked His supply in our lives to get us into that home, but we had to exercise our faith for that supply. Even after we moved into the house, we had to continue to call for the supply to come to us to maintain what He had moved us into.

If we would have tried to calculate where the money would come from for that home, we never would have been able to "figure it out". God doesn't want you to "figure out" your supply; He wants you to "walk it out", for we walk by faith and not by sight. We walk by faith and not by what we can figure out. We must trust the Lord with all our hearts, and not lean to our own understanding, not lean to our minds and what we can figure out and calculate.

Don't Limit Your Supply

God's supply can make all the difference in your income. Yes, we must walk in wisdom regarding our finances, but it must be the wisdom of the Word and not just human wisdom we rely on.

When you go to calculate your budget, you need to see what your income and expenses are, but don't let the budget you calculate become your limit. Have you noticed on your calculator that there's no "anointing" button, there's no "God's supply" button? Your calculator can't factor in God's supply, and your mind can't figure out God's supply, so make sure you don't let any budget become your limit or have the final word.

Rather, let your calculations show you how much faith you must exercise. For example, if your income is $50,000 a year, but you need $70,000 a year to accomplish some things that God has put in your heart, then the calculator has shown you that you need to exercise faith for the additional $20,000. Never let the calculator tell you that you can't have the $70,000 you need. You may see that you need an additional $20,000 and think, "I don't have enough faith to believe for $20,000!" Well, can you believe for $1,000? Then believe for $1,000 twenty times. Just learn that the calculator can't factor in God's resources. Let faith reach out for what can't be calculated.

CHAPTER 6

Avenues of Blessing

God's Word tells us that He will bless whatever we set our hand to. God will bless you in your profession and can cause you to reach the top in your field. He will use your job as an avenue to supply your needs, but your job is simply an avenue through which God will bless you; it is not your source and your provider.

When you realize that God is your Source and your Provider, then you won't become unsettled if your job or income changes. If you become unsettled when your job or income changes, it helps you locate where you've been placing your faith and what you've been trusting in.

Some professions allow for more increase than other professions. For example, a store owner is in a position to have more income than a sales clerk in that store. The level of responsibility is much higher for the store owner than the sales clerk, so his income will reflect that level of responsibility.

God will bless what you set your hand to, and if you're faithful, He can promote you to the top in your field. But if you want more income, you may have to set your hand to a job that allows for greater income. If you set your hand to a job where the top position pays only $20,000 a year, God can help you to rise to that top position. But if you want to make $60,000, then you have to set your hand to a profession that has that earning potential. He blesses what you set your hand to, but if you want more, you must set your hand to more.

There's a testimony of one man who was a popcorn vendor. He was faithful and diligent in his job, and God promoted him so that he rose to the top in his profession. He then realized that his profession could only allow for a certain level of income, so he began to talk to the Lord about a change in his profession. As he prayed and waited on the Lord, God started dealing with him about being a building contractor, for he had experience in that field. He changed his profession because there was more earning potential in the building industry than as a popcorn vendor. God was able to promote him to a higher level of income because of what he set his hand to and because of his faithfulness. God then promoted him from building contractor to a land developer, and because his level of responsibility increased, so did his income.

If you've risen to the top in your field, but you would still like to be at a higher level of income, then you may have to set your hand to a profession with a higher level of responsibility, so God's blessing can flow through that avenue to bring a greater supply of income.

Divine Ideas Bring Divine Supply

Remember that God has more than one avenue through which to bless you. So, don't decide that you can't have more than what your profession supplies.

I previously referred to a couple I've been friends with for years who God blessed to such a degree that they are worth millions. Years ago, the Lord called this man to help administrate a ministry that had a world-wide impact. Although the ministry paid him a fair salary, it wasn't the level of income he wanted to have. He told God, "I know I'm called to help this ministry, and I'm going to do that regardless of the amount of salary I'm paid, but because I need and want a higher income, I ask You to give me divine ideas regarding developing real estate that will cause a greater income."

God gave him divine ideas regarding developing real estate that were so creative that he was soon increasing to the point that he was making millions of dollars, all the while he was still the ministry administrator.

This is where a lot of people miss it. Because what God calls them to may not pay them the salary they want, they turn their back on their God-given call to pursue money. That's because they think their job is their source and their provision. When in truth, it's simply an avenue, not their source.

This friend of mine put God's call on his life first, not money. Then he used his faith to believe God for divine ideas to receive income through other avenues. Don't limit God to one avenue. He has many avenues through which He can bless you if you'll be faithful to do what He's told you to do, regardless of money. You can't figure out all the avenues through which God can move to supply you. You have to walk by faith to receive the flow of supply that comes through different avenues, but if you're going to pursue money instead of the plan of God for your life, you're going to limit God's supply to your life.

As I sat and listened to my friend tell of all the outstanding avenues of supply which God had blessed him through that made him a very wealthy man, he said, "I've never prayed and asked God for money. I always ask God for divine ideas!"

He knew that God's supply was attached to the divine idea.

If you'll be faithful to obey God, and to develop your spirit so that you're sensitive to the Holy Spirit, God will make you brilliant by the Holy Ghost, regardless of education. He will give you divine ideas that will be limitless in provision. Don't limit God!

Your job and income are not your source; they are simply avenues through which God will supply your needs. God is your Source and your Provider.

Don't attach your faith to the avenues God uses; your faith must be in Him. If you attach your faith to the avenue of your job, then your faith will falter if your job changes. Don't attach your faith to your paycheck, or your faith will falter if your paycheck decreases or stops. If you have attached your faith to God, then you won't be shaken if your job or paycheck changes because you know that God, who is your Source, hasn't changed. He remains the same, even when circumstances don't. God remains faithful even in the face of changes.

CHAPTER 7

Faith Reaches for More

Faith will reach out for more – more of God's supply and blessing. Put your hand to greater things and let greater supply flow into your life. If you're sitting back just waiting for God to bring His supply into your life, you'll never possess all He has for you. Faith is always moving and reaching out for more. It doesn't just wait for things to happen. Faith moves into what is happening; it moves into what God is doing.

Following God's Leading

Some Christians just sit, waiting to hear direction from God, but faith makes movement and listens for God's guidance and direction as it moves. Psalm 37:23 tells us, *"The STEPS of a good man are ordered by the Lord...."* If you want God to direct you, you have to make steps, so He can direct you. You can't steer a parked car. To guide a car in the direction you want it to go, it has to be moving. Likewise, to receive God's guidance, you have to be moving in some direction. Look what Luke wrote in Acts 16:6-9.

Acts 16:6-9
6   Now when they had gone throughout Phrygia and the region of Galatia, and WERE FORBIDDEN BY THE HOLY GHOST TO PREACH THE WORD IN ASIA,
7   After they were come to Mysia, they assayed to go into Bethynia: BUT THE SPIRIT SUFFERED THEM NOT.
8   And they passing by Mysia came down to Troas.
9   And a vision appeared to Paul in the night; there stood a man of Macedonia, and prayed him, saying, COME OVER INTO MACEDONIA, and help us.

Paul received direction because he was making movement, and as he made movement, God was able to direct him. Paul initially thought to preach the Word in Asia, but the Holy Ghost directed him away from there. So, evidently God didn't direct him into Asia, but Paul just purposed on his own to go. In this instance, Paul didn't sit back and wait for God to tell him where to preach; rather, he just went wherever the opportunity arose. He understood this about the way God leads. You need to make movement toward a particular direction, and if God doesn't want you to go that direction, He will tell you.

God didn't want Paul to preach in Asia, so the Spirit forbade him, and he obeyed. Paul didn't miss God by planning to go to Asia, but if he would have gone there after the Spirit told him not to, then he would have missed God.

We don't miss God unless we continue to go a particular direction after God has instructed us not to. If you aren't sure which direction to go, make movement toward some direction, and if God doesn't want you to go that direction, He'll give you a check in your spirit. Just don't go so far that you couldn't redirect your steps if He were to check you. As you start making movement in a direction, keep your spiritual antenna up so you can perceive the leading of the Lord, and if He guides you differently, follow His leading. Going in a certain direction without God's leading doesn't mean you've missed it and are out of God's will. You would only be out of God's will if you continued in a direction after He instructed you otherwise.

As we drive our vehicles, green lights don't instruct us to stop, but red lights do. We continue to drive until we come to a red light. Likewise, with the leading of God, He doesn't direct us primarily by green lights, but by red lights. Just keep making movement until God gives you a red light in your spirit, a leading to not go in that direction. When you get a check in your Spirit to not go a particular direction, you sense uneasiness within; you sense that you shouldn't go that direction.

That's what happened with Paul. He was going toward preaching in Asia, but he got a red light. When he got the red light, he stopped going in that direction, but he didn't just stop and sit; he endeavored to go into Bithynia. When God gives you a red light in your spirit, don't just sit inactive. Start going another direction.

When Paul started going a different direction into Bithynia, then again he got another red light from God, "...*the Spirit suffered them not*" (Acts 16:7). Paul still didn't miss God or get out of His will, for every time God gave him a red light, he followed it.

After Paul received a second red light not to go into Bithynia, he came down to Troas. While in Troas, further direction came to him. A vision of the night came to him, and a man of Macedonia said to him to come to Macedonia and help them, so Paul obeyed.

It wasn't until Paul endeavored to go to three different regions that he had the vision. Paul understood that to receive God's leading, he needed to make movement.

Faith never sits inactive, but it makes movement. Faith is ever pressing forward and will follow the leading of God along the way as it is given. Faith will change directions when God leads you to. Paul wasn't failing because he changed his plans three times; rather, he was moving in faith, he was moving with God.

CHAPTER 8

The Greater One in You

Genesis 39:1-6

1   And Joseph was brought down to Egypt; and Potiphar, an officer of Pharaoh, captain of the guard, an Egyptian, bought him of the hands of the Ishmaelites, which had brought him down thither.

2   And the Lord was with Joseph, and he was a prosperous man; and he was in the house of his master the Egyptian.

3   And his master saw that the Lord was with him, and that the Lord made all that he did to prosper in his hand.

4   And Joseph found grace in his sight, and he served him: and he made him overseer over his house, and all that he put into his hand.

5   And it came to pass from the time that he had made him overseer in his house, and over all that he had, that the Lord blessed the Egyptian's house for Joseph's sake; and the blessing of the Lord was upon all that he had in the house, and it was full.

6   And he left all he had in Joseph's hand; and he knew not aught he had, save the bread which he did eat. And Joseph was a goodly person, and well-favored.

As a young man, Joseph's brothers sold him out of jealousy to men traveling to Egypt. When Joseph was brought to Egypt, he was sold as a slave to Potiphar, an officer of Pharaoh.

When we look at Genesis 39:2, we read, "*And the Lord was with Joseph....*" Joseph was prosperous because the Lord was with him, and because of this, everything Joseph did prospered.

Joseph's station in life had sunk to the lowest position; he became a slave, and it was his own brothers who sold him into that position. Even as a slave, he was prosperous because the Lord was with him. Because Joseph didn't allow himself to be made bitter by what others wrongfully did to him, he ended up serving alongside Pharaoh.

It doesn't matter what your social standing in life may be or what your background is. What matters in life is that the Lord is with you, and He is in you, if you're born again!

In fact, the born again believer has more available to him than Joseph had. The Old Testament saints were God's people, but they weren't born again because Jesus hadn't yet died and paid the price for their sin. They didn't have the life and nature of God in them as those of us who are born again. They weren't the temple of the Holy Ghost like we are. God was with them, but He wasn't in them.

True prosperity is having God with you and on the inside of you. Since He's in you, you can yield yourself to Him and allow Him to dominate through you. When He gets His way through you, He will make all you do to prosper.

Live mindful of the greater One who's on the inside of you. Live mindful of the God who supplies all your needs. Don't live mindful of the need; rather, live mindful of the God who supplies all your needs.

CHAPTER 9

Taking God's Paths

Ephesians 2:10, Amplified
For we are God's [own] handiwork (His workmanship), recreated in Christ Jesus, [born anew] that we may do those good works which God predestined (planned beforehand) for us [taking paths which He prepared ahead of time], that we should walk in them [living the good life which he prearranged and made ready for us to live].

Paul tells us in this passage that we are God's own handiwork. That handiwork is the recreation of our spirits. When we were born again, God didn't heal our old spirit, but He created a new spirit within us. Our new spirit has God's own nature and God's life in it; our spirit is born again.

Ephesians 2:10 (Amplified Bible) tells us that our spirit is born anew so that we can do those good works which God predestined and planned beforehand for us. God has a plan for every person. There is a plan that God has for us to accomplish.

The plans that God has called us to accomplish have to be funded. Most of the work that we are called to do in the earth requires finances, but in Ephesians 2:10, God shows us that He has already prepared everything for us that we will ever need. It reads, "*...that we may do those good works which God predestined (planned beforehand) for us [taking paths which HE PREPARED ahead of time], that we should walk in them [living the good life which HE PREARRANGED AND MADE READY FOR US to live].*"

The paths He has for us to walk are "prepared" for us. He's already prepared and arranged for us everything we're going to need on these paths. The supply to carry out the good works He has planned for us are on the paths. As long as we stay on the paths He planned for us, the supply will be on those paths for us to gather up with our faith.

If we veer away from the paths, we veer away from the supply. We must stay with God's plan to enjoy the fullness of supply He has for us. Much difficulty will arise in our life when we get away from God's plan. On the paths of God's will for our life is all the supply we will need.

If proper supply and provision have eluded you, check two areas of your life. Number one, make sure you're walking out the paths that God has prepared for you. Number two, make sure you're continually releasing your faith in God's supply, calling His supply into your life.

If you're not sure that you're walking out His paths for your life, take time to wait before God, praying in other tongues until you have clarity in your spirit of His plan.

Don't Forfeit Your Supply

Hebrews 4:3 (Amplified Bible) reads, "... *[His] works had been completed and prepared [and waiting for all who would believe] from the foundation of the world*." This passage tells us of how God had so fully prepared for His Hebrew children that He delivered out of Egypt. Although they failed to believe God and refused to enter the promise land, God still had fully prepared everything for them. Notice that the supply they needed was, "...*completed and prepared [and WAITING FOR ALL WHO WOULD BELIEVE]*...."

God's supply is waiting for one thing – your faith! It's waiting for all who will believe.

Although the Hebrews didn't exercise their faith and believe God to receive their supply, the supply was still waiting on them. Hebrews 4:5, the Amplified Bible, tells us "...*they FORFEITED THEIR PART in it....*"

If a baseball team forfeits a game, it's because they didn't have enough players to show up to play the game. Hebrews 4:5 tells us that the Hebrew children forfeited their part in what God had prepared for them. They failed to "show up" with their faith, and they forfeited what belonged to them all along.

Forty years later, after that first generation had died off, the next generation exercised faith for what the first generation had forfeited, and they moved into the supply that had been waiting all along.

God's supply is waiting for your faith. It's not enough that the supply is prepared by God. Faith has to lay hold of it.

Because that first generation refused to move forward into God's plan, they suffered unnecessary hardship and difficulties. They faced tragedies and crises that God never intended for them to face. When Christians veer away from God's plan and veer away from faith, they face unnecessary hardships and difficulties. They face tragedies and crises that God never intended for them to face.

That generation that God delivered out of Egypt forfeited God's supply for them because they didn't stay with God's plan. But when the second generation moved with God's plan, they moved into God's supply.

God's supply is with His plan. Stay with His plan to stay with His supply. But even when you're walking out God's plan, you must exercise your faith. God's supply won't fall on you automatically just because you're in God's will; you must exercise your faith for

God's supply. With words of faith, you lay hold of God's supply. God's supply can't be found just anywhere, it is with His plan.

Be Where God Told You to Be

Genesis 22 tells the incident of how God proved Abraham's faith by telling him to offer Isaac as a sacrifice.

Genesis 22:2, 3 & 9
2   And he said, Take now thy son, thine only son Isaac, whom thou lovest, and get thee into the land of Moriah; and offer him there for a burnt offering upon one of the mountains WHICH I WILL TELL THEE OF.
3   And Abraham rose early in the morning, and saddled his ass, and took two of his young men with him, and Isaac his son, and clave the wood for the burnt offering, and rose up, and WENT UNTO THE PLACE OF WHICH GOD HAD TOLD HIM.
9   AND THEY CAME TO THE PLACE WHICH GOD HAD TOLD HIM OF; and Abraham built the alter THERE...

God didn't only instruct Abraham to offer up his son as a sacrifice, but he also told him the exact location of where he was to make the sacrifice. It was a three day journey to get there.

After Abraham reached the mountain, he built an altar, bound his son, and prepared to offer him as a sacrifice, but further instructions came. As he took the knife to slay Isaac, God spoke and stopped him, saying that now He knew that he feared God.

Genesis 22:13 & 14 tells us, "*And Abraham lifted up his eyes, and looked, and behold behind him a ram caught in a thicket by his horns: and Abraham went and took the ram, and offered him up for a burnt offering in the stead of his son (KJV). So Abraham called the name of that place the Lord will provide. And it is said to this day, on the Mount of the Lord it will be provided*" (Amplified).

What if Abraham had decided that he could make the sacrifice on just any mountain, maybe one closer to where he was living? Why go to the one that took a three day journey? Why not go to a more convenient location? Why was it so important that Abraham go to the mountain God told him to?

The mountain where God told him to go to was where the supply was; that's where the provision was; that's where the ram was. The supply wasn't at every mountain in the region; it was on the mountain where God told him to go to. God spoke to him on that mountain. God supplied for him on that mountain. He couldn't have gone just anywhere and had the supply of a ram. God spoke to Abraham, and God supplied for him in the place where He told him to be. The supply for your life isn't just anywhere; it is where God tells you to be. God's supply is with God's plan.

CHAPTER 10

An Easy Supply

God has a plan for every one of His children. He has good works for each to accomplish while on this earth, but God's plan is going to require God's supply. That is why it is so important for Christians to renew their minds with the truth that we find in Philippians 4:19, "*My God shall supply all your need according to his riches in glory by Christ Jesus.*"

Proverbs 23:7 tells us, "*For as he thinketh in his heart, so is he....*" It is important what you think regarding God's supply, for you're going to "have" in line with how you think. If you think that supply is hard for you, it will be hard. If you think supply for you is minimal, it will be minimal. Your thinking limits or allows your supply. Your thinking is the gatekeeper, letting supply in or keeping supply out.

One day, someone handed me some money as an offering. When they did, God spoke to me and said, "Give that money to Grant (Grant is our youngest son who was about 9 years old at the time) and tell him that My supply for him is easy. It's not a hard supply, it's an easy supply."

It matters that we think right toward God's supply. His supply is abundant, and it flows easily to us. God is not a withholder, He is a giver. God will never withhold supply from you. He has already provided it, but it takes faith to receive it.

If you have a financial need that arises, the money is already on the earth. Heaven isn't going to send the money down, but God will influence people to give to you, or He will open doors through which the supply will come. The Word tells us that God will give to us through the hands of men. It may take time for that supply to show up, but that's because other people are involved.

The enemy may seek to hinder the progress of that supply moving to your life, but as you continue to exercise your faith, it will overcome any hindrance.

Just because the enemy may seek to hinder and slow down the supply from reaching your life, that doesn't mean that the supply is hard or diminished. The supply is from God, and He has supplied it freely, and it is abundant.

Any opposition is from the enemy. Don't blame or find fault with the supply. Don't blame or find fault with God. The enemy is to blame for any opposition, not God or the supply. Know this – the supply is easy, the supply is abundant, and it belongs to you, but the supply requires your faith so that no opposition can withhold it from you.

Romans 4:17 tells us how faith operates. It tells us what faith does. Faith *"...CALLETH those things which be not as though they were."* Faith has to call for the supply that is yours to come to you. Whatever you may need, there's a supply, so call it! Tell it to come to you!

Many are waiting for God to send their supply, but the supply is waiting for you to call it. Faith's job is to call. It is not faith's job to worry, figure out or calculate. It is faith's job to call.

How long do you have to call it? You have to call it until it shows up. Don't try to figure out how it is going to come, or where it is going to come from, just call it! The more you call it, the more you'll have it. The less you call it, the less you'll have it.

The supply of God is yours. Every need that you will ever face has a supply, and it is faith that receives that supply. So call the supply, and tell it to come to you. It's waiting for the call of faith.

PART II
ELIJAH & THE WIDOW WOMAN

CHAPTER 11

Elijah and the Widow Woman

God has something to say to us through His Word during times of economic hardship. His Word is for every season in life that we may face. His Word is our answer and our help no matter what may be going on in the world around us. While economic hardship may fall hard on the world, our situation is to be one of overwhelming supply and blessing as we continue to walk by faith and follow the leading of His Spirit. Let's look at a passage of scripture that shows God's overwhelming supply.

I Kings 17:1-16
1   And Elijah the Tishbite, who was of the inhabitants of Gilead, said unto Ahab, As the Lord God of Israel liveth, before whom I stand, there shall not be dew nor rain these years, but according to my word.
2   And the word of the Lord came unto him, saying,
3   Get thee hence, and turn thee eastward, and hide thyself by the brook Cherith, that is before Jordan.
4   And it shall be, that thou shalt drink of the brook; and I have commanded the ravens to feed thee there.
5   So he went and did according unto the word of the Lord; for he went and dwelt by the brook Cherith, that is before Jordan.
6   And the ravens brought him bread and flesh in the morning, and bread and flesh in the evening; and he drank of the brook.
7   And it came to pass after a while, that the brook dried up, because there had been no rain.
8   And the word of the Lord came unto him, saying,

9 Arise, get thee to Zarephath, which belongth to Zidon, and dwell there: behold, I have commanded a widow woman there to sustain thee.

10 So he arose and went to Zarephath. And when he came to the gate of the city, behold, the widow woman was there gathering of sticks: and he called to her, and said, Fetch me, I pray thee, a little water in a vessel , that I may drink.

11 And as she was going to fetch it, he called her, and said, Bring me, I pray thee, a morsel of bread in thine hand.

12 And she said, As the Lord thy God liveth, I have not a cake, but an handful of meal in a barrel, and a little oil in a cruse: and, behold, I am gathering two sticks, that I may go in and dress it for me and my son, that we may eat it, and die.

13 And Elijah said unto her, Fear not; go and do as thou hast said: but make me thereof a little cake first, and bring it unto me, and after make for thee and thy son.

14 For thus saith the Lord God of Israel, The barrel of meal shall not waste, neither shall the cruse of oil fail, until the day that the Lord sendeth rain upon the earth.

15 And she went and did according to the saying of Elijah: and she, and he, and her house, did eat many days.

16 And the barrel of meal wasted not, neither did the cruse of oil fail, according to the word of the Lord, which he spake by Elijah.

God told Elijah, "*...I have commanded a widow woman there to sustain thee.*" Notice who God chose to use to bring a supply to the prophet of God – a widow woman! She was not only a widow woman, but she was a widow woman with a child! Not only was she a widow woman with a child, but she was a starving widow woman with a child! Her own needs were acute!

When the man of God needed a supply, God did not command an influential person of society, a businessman, or someone of obvious means – He chose a starving widow woman with a child. God did not choose the wealthy to supply His man; He chose the available.

When God chose this starving widow woman with a child, He was choosing an avenue so that all would know that it was God's ability that accomplished the supply and not the person's ability to accomplish it.

What's in Your Spirit?

When Elijah needed a miracle to sustain him, God sent him to receive his supply through someone else who needed a miracle.

God told Elijah, "...*I HAVE COMMANDED a widow woman there to sustain thee.*" God had already given a command to the woman, but she does not act as if she knows anything about that command when Elijah arrives. There was this command that God had assigned to her life that her mind had not yet processed. It took the help of someone else who knew God's voice to draw out of the widow's heart what God had put in her heart. Elijah helped her to identify and act on God's command for her life.

There are things your own spirit knows that your mind has not processed yet. Your own spirit knows things that your mind doesn't know yet.

As a pastor, I believe that God gives me the utterances to speak that which will help the people to identify and draw out what God has already put in their hearts, calling up the things God has deposited in their spirits.

Faith Will Do Whatever it Takes

God had a supply for Elijah through someone who did not look like they had a supply to give.

Those who are in need will, many times, automatically dismiss themselves from bringing a supply when a need is presented. But God knew of this widow woman's acute needs, and He didn't see her needs as a valid reason to dismiss her from bringing a supply when His prophet needed a supply. In fact, He laid the command for the prophet's supply on her.

There must have been something about this woman that caused God to choose her to be a supply to the prophet. We know it was not her wealth and abundance, for she did not have that. Why was she chosen?

Her faith is the reason God chose her. How do we know that she had faith? We can tell she had faith by seeing what she was doing when Elijah arrived in her city – she was gathering sticks. "*So he arose and went to Zarephath. And when he came to the gate of the city, behold, the widow woman was there gathering of sticks...*" (I Kings 17:10). What does the gathering of sticks have to do with faith? This woman did not lie in her bed and bemoan the fact that she and her son were starving. She was not home crying about the fact that there was no work and no food to be found anywhere. Rather, she was out, scouring the city for what she needed. That is faith. Faith will do whatever it takes to get the job done.

James tells us that, "*...faith without works* (corresponding actions) *is dead*" (James 2:20). If you have faith, you will do something; you will make movement. To be inactive toward a need is to lack faith.

James goes on to tell us, "*For as the body without the spirit is dead, so faith without works is dead also*" (James 2:26). It is the spirit of man that gives life and movement to the body; without the spirit his body is dead and gets no further movement. Likewise, when there are no works of faith, faith becomes dead and gets no movement. What the spirit is to the body, works or action is to faith. If there are no actions of faith, the faith dies.

This woman was acting in faith whether she realized it or not. In her great need, she was still making movement. This is the point where many fail. When lack shows up, when a job is lost, many will just resign themselves to lack and quit looking for their supply. But God has something better for you if you'll keep exercising your faith, keep making faith movements, and keep putting a demand on the supply of God for your life. Jobs may fail, business connections may fail, but faith never fails! Feed your faith on God's Word, express your faith through speaking God's Word, and act your faith by seeking out your supply.

Look what Jesus said in Matthew 6:26. "*Look at the birds of the air; they neither sow nor reap nor gather into barns, and yet your heavenly Father keeps feeding them. Are you not worth much more than they?*" (Amplified).

God feeds the birds. How does He feed them? Does he just throw seeds and worms into their nest every morning? No, He has stocked the earth with a full supply of provision for the birds, but the birds still have to get out of their nests and go gather up their supply from God.

God is not going to just throw your supply into your bank account every morning. You have to go out and gather up the supply that God has assigned to your life. That is what faith will do. It will go out and gather up the supply. Faith does not wait for the supply to find you. Faith goes out and gathers it up.

That is what this widow woman was doing. She was out gathering up her supply. She was moving in faith. The gathering of sticks did not look supernatural. It was probably something she did every day. Faith does not always look very spectacular. Sometimes it looks just as common as the gathering of sticks, but it is still faith!

When Elijah arrived in the city, she is the only one spoken of as being at the city gate gathering sticks. Everybody else must have been at home, lamenting their situation in the time of famine. Others had resigned themselves to starvation, but not this woman. She is out gathering supply!

It was when she was out gathering, that her miracle partner walked through the city gates and found her. If she had stayed at home, resigned to starvation, she could have missed her divine connection with the prophet of God; he might not have found her.

Many miss their miracle because they sit in their sad situation, resigning themselves to lack instead of getting out and looking for their supply. Faith makes movement! Faith does not sit idly by, hoping that God will toss their supply into their nest! If you want your supply from God, at least do what the birds do every day. Get out of your nest and go gather up your supply! It will not find you while you're sitting in front of the television; get up and go search it out!

Think of the scene Elijah saw when he walked into the city. He does find this widow woman with God's command on her life to be his supply, but when he finds her, she is gathering sticks. Those sticks she was gathering were the scraps of a city destitute. She didn't look like she had a supply for him, but she did!

Not only was the widow woman acting in faith by gathering sticks, but Elijah had to act in faith when he saw the one God had commanded to be his supply living off scraps. Elijah did not start operating out of the mental arena when he saw the condition of this woman. He did not start reasoning to himself, thinking that there was no way for this widow woman to be his avenue of supply. Elijah understood that it is not circumstances that determine provision, but faith.

I Kings 17:10-12
10 ...And when he came to the gate of the city, behold, the widow woman was there gathering of sticks: and he called to her, and said, Fetch me, I pray thee, a little water in a vessel, that I may drink.
11 And as she was going to fetch it, he called to her, and said, Bring me, I pray thee, a morsel of bread in thine hand.
12 And she said, As the Lord thy God liveth, I have not a cake, but an handful of meal in a barrel, and a little oil in a cruse: and, behold, I am gathering two sticks that I may go in and dress it for me and my son, that we may eat it, and die.

When Elijah needed a miracle to sustain him, God sent him to receive his supply through someone else who needed a miracle.

What was the widow's part in this miracle? To act on what God commanded her through the prophet.

What was Elijah's part in this miracle? He had to locate the woman to whom God had given the command. Did you know that Elijah could not have gone to just any woman in the city and received the supply he needed? He had to go to the one whom God had commanded to bring his supply.

Likewise, you cannot just go any direction in life and receive God's supply. You have to go where God tells you to go; you have to follow His plan for your life. God's supply is connected to God's plan.

You veer away from God's plan, and you veer away from God's supply.

Pressing Past Hardship

Elijah commanded the widow woman, "...*Fetch me, I pray thee, a little water in a vessel that I may drink. And as she was going to fetch it, he called to her, and said, Bring me, I pray thee, a morsel of bread in thine hand*" (I Kings 17:10 & 11).

When Elijah just asked for water, she immediately started to go get it. Getting him water was no hard thing for her to do. How simple and routine this request sounds to a mother who is used to taking care of a child, but this is no routine request – it is the beginning of her miracle! It does not sound very spectacular. It sounds too simple to be her answer, but it is the first step toward her miracle.

She easily goes on her way to fetch the water, for that does not take much faith. Water was a public resource. It would cost her nothing to obey that request. But then Elijah calls out further instruction to her, "Bring me a morsel of bread." This request was harder. God's requests can get harder on the flesh sometimes, can't they? Why was this request harder? The water was a *public* resource, but to bring him bread would mean she would have to dive into her *personal* resources. This request stopped her in her tracks, for this request dug deeper into her situation of need.

Now she turns back from going to get water for Elijah to tell him how dire her own personal needs are. I Kings 17:12, "*And she said, As the Lord thy God liveth, I have not a cake, but an handful of meal in a barrel, and a little oil in a cruse: and behold, I am gathering two sticks, that I may go in and dress it for me and my son, that we may eat it, and die.*"

When the prophet hears how acute her need is, he does not dismiss her from his request; he only gets more emphatic! Why? He knows that if she dismisses herself from fulfilling his request because she has needs herself, she will dismiss herself from her miracle. The prophet did not just have his miracle in mind; he had her miracle in mind, too. Her need did not dismiss her from the supply she was to bring to the man of God; it only made it more necessary for her to bring her supply.

Having a need does not dismiss you from bringing a supply; it only makes it more of a necessity that you bring a supply.

To the casual onlooker or to someone with an unrenewed mind, it might look as though Elijah's urgent command for the widow woman was self-serving, that he only had his need in mind. But he knows that he must have her cooperation if she is to receive her miracle.

It looks as though Elijah's command to bring him some bread to eat is only adding to her hardship. But when God instructs us to do something, in the natural it may look like He is pressing us further into hardship, but He is really just pressing us past hardship.

Resist Fear

When Elijah requested her to bring him water, she went to fetch it without an argument, but as she was going, he called to her to also bring him some bread. It was this request that stopped her in her tracks. She quit making progress to fulfill the command. She stopped moving forward and returned to the prophet to tell him of her dire circumstances.

I Kings 17:12 & 13
12 And she said, As the Lord thy God liveth, I have not a cake, but an handful of meal in a barrel, and a little oil in a cruse:

and, behold, I am gathering two sticks, that I may go in and dress it for me and my son, that we may eat it, and die.
13 And Elijah said unto her, FEAR NOT; GO AND DO...

Elijah knew what was keeping her from moving forward to fulfill the command the man of God gave her — it was fear!

The spirit of fear will seek to attach itself to us because fear paralyzes faith. Fear paralyzed this widow woman because it was keeping her from moving forward and fulfilling the plan given her. If fear is yielded to, all forward movement will stop. Fear will cause someone to go in reverse, moving in a backward direction until all progress and increase is lost. Fear is not just a feeling; it is a spirit.

Second Timothy 1:7 tells us, "*For God hath not given us the SPIRIT OF FEAR; but of power, and of love, and of a sound mind.*" When the spirit of fear raises its head, speak to it. Tell that spirit to leave you.

"*Resist the devil and he will flee from you*" (James 4:7). Fear is of the devil; resist it!

How do you resist? You resist by speaking to it! Speak God's Word to it. Tell the enemy, "God hath not given me the spirit of fear; but God has given me the spirit of power, of love, and of a sound mind."

God is not dealing with you through fear. He is not leading you through fear. Fear is an enemy. Resist it! Fear seeks to deceive you into thinking that what it threatens is true. It suggests something to you that is believable, but do not listen to that spirit! The enemy will gain the advantage if you listen to him, but refuse to listen to him. Do not entertain thoughts of fear.

If you believe what the enemy tells you, he will steal from you everything God has ever blessed you with. When thoughts of fear come, answer them saying, "Those aren't my thoughts. I will not believe them."

One minister tells of a time when a spirit of fear attacked him. That spirit said to the minister, "See, you're afraid. Look at your body. Your hands are shaking. You're afraid!"

The minister replied, "No, devil. I am not afraid. My body isn't the real me. My spirit is the real me, and my spirit isn't shaking!"

Answer fear! Do not entertain thoughts of fear! Refuse to believe what fear tells you.

Answer Fear

When the Israeli army was faced with Goliath, the Bible tells us that the Israeli army hid themselves. They hid in fear when they heard his words.

David fought and defeated Goliath because he was not afraid of him. When the Israeli army heard Goliath's threats, they hid themselves, but when David heard his threats, he answered him every time!

Do not let fear have the last word. Answer it!

David conquered Goliath because he first conquered fear. To conquer any giant, you must first conquer fear. How do you do that? Answer fear with the Word of God.

Keep Acting on the Word

Elijah knew that if this widow woman was to receive her miracle, she was going to have to press past fear. Famine was not this woman's great enemy; fear was. Fear wanted her to not act on God's command.

When fear comes, keep acting on the Word of God. Keep doing what God told you to do. How do we overcome the enemy of fear? By being a doer of the Word. James 2:26 tells us, "...*faith without works* (corresponding actions) *is dead.*" Faith is released through what you say and what you do. Fear seeks to paralyze you from doing the Word, but you overcome that fear by doing the Word.

The devil deceives many people into thinking that everything will change for them if they will just believe God. But believing God involves acting on the Word. If you're not acting on the Word, you're not believing. Faith is an act! Faith is not just a belief, it is an act. It is not enough to just believe God. The Bible tells us that the demons believe and tremble. Believing is not complete without acting on the Word.

The Word doesn't tell us we'll have what we believe. Jesus said, "...*he shall have whatsoever he SAITH*" (Mark 11:23).

Romans 10:10 reads, "*For with the heart man believeth unto righteousness; AND with the mouth confession* (saying) *is made unto salvation* (manifestation)." It takes believing with the heart and saying with the mouth for faith to work.

Hearing the Word will cause you to believe, but *speaking* the Word will cause you to receive. That's why more people believe than receive, because receiving takes acting – you must speak it. You don't have to act on the Word to believe, but you do have to act on the Word to receive. When you're speaking the Word, you are acting.

Faith is an act. Act on the Word, and overcome fear.

If this widow woman was to receive her miracle, she was going to have to act on the word of the man of God in the face of fear.

In a time of economic hardship in a nation, fear is prevalent, and that spirit of fear operating in the world will try to get in the church and in the life of the believer. The way to keep that fear out is to act on the Word and not in fear.

As we act on the Word, the Gospel will continue to be funded, and the plan of God in the earth will not be hindered.

The Divine Order of Supply

First Kings 17:13 reads, "*And Elijah said unto her, Fear not; go and do as thou hast said: but make me thereof a little cake FIRST, and bring it unto me, and AFTER make for thee and for thy son.*"

Elijah told her to make him a cake *first* and bring it to him, *then* make one for her and her son. Every miracle has a divine order of events. God is the One who determines that divine order, not us. When He gives us a divine order of events to fulfill, we are not authorized to change that divine order. The divine order for this woman's miracle was that she make a cake for the man of God first.

If you want to receive God's supply for your life, you have to do what He says in the order He gives it. To change the order of the command is to veer from the plan of God. To have divine results, we must *fully* follow God's command to us without interjecting our opinion. God is always right, and His plan is always perfect. It needs no adjustments from us.

In the natural, she thought she did not have enough to give to the man of God, but if she gave to him first, she would have enough.

Some Christians think they do not have enough money to give their tithes, but if they give their tithes first, before anything else, they will always have enough to give their tithes. God's divine order is that we give our tithes (the first tenth) of all our increase to Him before we pay anything else. To change this divine order is to veer from the plan of God. To veer from God's plan is to veer away from God's supply. We must obey God's divine order if we are to receive all we need from the Lord.

The end or the outcome of a situation is determined by what went first. If God is put first, then He can be involved in how a situation ends and turns out. If we do not put Him first, then He cannot be involved in the outcome the way He wants to be.

Be Quick to Obey

After the widow woman tells the prophet how desperate her circumstances are, Elijah instructs her, "*...Fear not; go and do as thou hast said: but make me thereof a little cake FIRST, and BRING IT UNTO ME, and AFTER make for thee and thy son*" (First Kings 17:13).

The prophet not only tells her to make his cake first, but to bring it to him before she starts on her own. He did not want the cake she made for him to just sit around while she made a cake for her and her son. He knew that the quicker she acted on what he was telling her to do, the less opportunity the enemy had to talk her out of obeying what he commanded her, and the less time she would have to reason out in her mind against the command.

The quicker you obey what God tells you to do, the less time you have to reason against God's command, and the less time the enemy has to try to talk you out of obedience.

The prophet told her to make his cake first and to *bring it to him*. Do not eat it! Bring it to him! The prophet was not going to follow her to her house and collect the cake she made him. She was to bring it to him.

It is the job of the sheep to *bring* their tithes and offering to the local church. It is not the job of the pastor to go to their house to collect it. It is their job to *bring* it to the church. Bring the tithe to the storehouse! Do not eat it! Obey quickly so the enemy does not have a chance to get you to eat what should have been brought to the local church.

Many *intend* to obey, but take too long, and then the devil talks them out of it. It is not enough to intend to obey, but obedience must be followed through; it must be completed.

Go Fetch It!

Elijah told the woman to go and *fetch* him water, to go and make him a cake, then bring it to him.

This sounds a lot like what we are instructed to do in Malachi 3:10, "*BRING ye all the tithes into the storehouse, that there may be meat* (supply) *in mine house....*" We are told to bring our tithes to the storehouse, which is the local church, the place where the sheep come to get their spiritual food. Why are they to bring their tithe? So that there will be meat (supply) in the local church.

It needs to matter to the sheep if there is enough meat (supply) for the local church to operate on. Sheep must be taught to be interested and involved in making sure that the local church has the funds they need to keep functioning.

Where would the sheep be without their local church? Without a pastor the sheep would faint and be scattered (Matthew 9:36). This must be taught to the sheep.

To talk about the local church's need for funds is not doubt or greed. The local church is a family, and it takes money for every family to operate. The local church is no different.

Pastors need to teach the sheep the role giving places in the life of the sheep and in the funding of the local church. If the church falls behind financially, the pastor can let the people know, so they can exercise their faith and rally financially to meet the need.

Proverbs 13:22, reads, "...*the wealth of the sinner is laid up for the just." But since it is "laid up*", you are going to have to go fetch it! It will not just automatically appear in your hands.

Continued Obedience

What if this widow woman would have made the cake for the prophet, fully intending to take it to him, but then heard her starving son crying for food? What if she had then reasoned that her child needed it worse than a grown man? She would have forfeited her miracle. Then her son would have starved to death, and it would not be because of lack, but because of her disobedience.

When it seems like you do not have enough, all kinds of things will cry out to you. Unpaid bills, late mortgages, overdue car payments will start crying out loud, wanting to be fed, but don't take the portion that belongs to God and feed it to what's crying. If you do, you will forfeit your miracle, then you will fail financially, and it will not be because of lack, but because of disobedience.

For the widow woman, making the cake for the prophet and bringing it to him in the face of her own great need was the act of obedience needed if she was to receive her miracle. God has a miracle for us, but it needs our act of obedience.

One act of obedience our miracle needs is to bring the tithes and offerings to our local church. When God requests this of us, it is not so He can press us *into* further hardship, but so He can press us *past* hardship. Don't let the reasonings of the mind cause you to disobey what God has said. Reasoning is doubt in disguise. Do not reason against the Word of God. It is your answer! Agree with God's Word by acting on it.

I Kings 17:13-16
13 And Elijah said unto her, Fear not; go and do as thou hast said: but make me thereof a little cake first, and bring it unto me, and after make for thee and for thy son.
14 For thus saith the Lord God of Israel, The barrel of meal shall not waste, neither shall the cruse of oil fail, until the day that the Lord sendeth rain upon the earth.
15 And she went and did according to the saying of Elijah: and she, and he, and her house, did eat many days.
16 And the barrel of meal wasted not, neither did the cruse of oil fail, according to the Word of the Lord, which he spake by Elijah.

When the widow woman obeyed the man of God, famine was over in her house. She obeyed the prophet by making his cake first, bringing it to him; then, after that she would make a cake for herself and her son. She did not just do what Elijah said on that first day, for he stayed in her home many days (the margin of my Bible says he stayed for one year). But *every* day she did what he had said to her on the day he arrived. Every day she made his cake first, brought it to him; then, she made one for her and her son. The miracle of her oil and her meal that did not run out was not just for her to *consume* it, but it was a miracle that had to be *shared* with the man of God if it was going to continue. If she would have ever stopped sharing of her increase with the man of God, her miracle would have dried up.

Can you lose a miracle? Absolutely! Peter received a miracle when he walked on the water to Jesus, but he lost a miracle when he became distracted by the wind that led him to doubt. A miracle must not only be received, but it must be maintained by continuing to act on God's Word in faith.

The supply of many Christians has dried up because they stopped being a supply to their local church financially when they were faced with their own financial need. This widow woman made giving to God's man a lifestyle. She did not just give occasionally to him, but she saw that her own supply was connected to her faithfulness to give to him first. Occasional obedience will never succeed in times of need. It is a lifestyle of obedience to God's Word, a lifestyle of giving that will receive its supply.

Those with an unrenewed mind may become offended if more than one offering is received in a service, or think that giving one time should bring a lifetime change, but this woman's continued giving secured for her a continued miracle.

Every time we are given an opportunity to give in our local church, we are receiving an opportunity to secure a continual supply. Giving does not earn God's supply, but it releases God's supply, causing the supply to flow. Just as flipping on a light switch causes electrical power to flow, giving in faith flips the switch to God's supply, causing it to flow.

The Place to Sow

Before God sent Elijah to this widow woman, God was sustaining him through ravens that were bringing him bread and meat twice a day (I King's 17:1-7). When this widow woman needed a miracle, God did not send ravens to supply this widow woman with food. When she needed a miracle, God sent her a man of God to sow into. God provided her with a place to sow. When you need a financial miracle, God does the same thing for you; He gives you a place to sow. The foremost place you should sow your finances is in your local church. That is the best ground for you to sow into.

My father is a cotton and wheat farmer in southwest Oklahoma. Whenever it is planting season, seed is abundant. He can go into most any Feed & Supply Store and get his seed to plant. But what is harder to come by is good, fertile ground.

Money is your seed. Money for sowing is easy to come by. You can easily do a number of things to get some money to sow. But what is harder to find is good ground to sow that money into.

It is good and right to give offerings to ministries other than your local church, but that should be done only after you have first given tithes and offerings to your own local church.

Your local church is the most important ministry in your life because that is the ministry that is there and available to your life in a personal way.

Recognize the places to sow that God has provided for you in your life, then plant your seed. Be faithful to make sowing a lifestyle, and you will receive a continual harvest of God's supply in your life as you exercise your faith.

PART III
PROSPERITY TRUTHS

CHAPTER 12

Honor

Proverbs 3:9 & 10
9 HONOUR the Lord with thy substance, and will the FIRST-FRUITS (TITHE) of all thine increase:
10 So shall thy barns be filled with plenty, and thy presses shall burst out with new wine.

This scripture shows us what is at the heart of our giving – honor. Many turn giving into strictly a money issue, but giving is really an honor issue; it's about what you honor. For Christians, our honor is to be toward God; therefore, we show our honor through our giving.

You can look at someone's checkbook and see what he honors. People always fund what they honor. *"For where your treasure is, there will your heart be also"* (Matthew 6:21).

Acts 10:1-6
1 There was a certain man in Caesarea called Cornelius, a centurion of the band called the Italian band,
2 A devout man, and one that feared God with all his house, which gave much alms to the people, and prayed to God always.
3 He saw in a vision evidently about the ninth hour of the day an angel of God coming in to him, and saying unto him, Cornelius.
4 And when he looked on him, he was afraid, and said, What is it Lord? And he said unto him, Thy prayers and thine alms are come up for a memorial before God.

5   And now send men to Joppa, and call for one Simon, whose surname is Peter:

6   He lodgeth with one Simon a tanner, whose house is by the sea side: he shall tell thee what thou oughtest to do.

Cornelius did as the angel instructed him and sent for Peter to come to his house. By the time Peter arrived, Cornelius had gathered his family and his friends together to hear all that Peter had to say to them. As Peter spoke, the Holy Ghost fell on them, and they were all born again and filled with the Holy Ghost (Acts 10:44-48).

This is the first time the Gospel is preached to the Gentiles, and Cornelius was the first Gentile to receive the Gospel. He and all those gathered in his home were born again and filled with the Spirit with the evidence of speaking in other tongues.

What was so outstanding about this man that made him the avenue for the Gospel's entrance to the Gentiles? Act 10:2 answers that. "*A devout man, and one that FEARED* (REVERENCED) *God with all his house, which GAVE MUCH ALMS TO the people, and PRAYED TO GOD ALWAYS.*" Again, we see that when someone reverences and honors God, it shows up in the way they give.

Cornelius' giving did not purchase anything from God, but it expressed his heart and opened his heart to receive the greater things God had for him.

Giving is an honor issue. Your money stays on the earth, but your honor goes to God.

God has declared that the first ten percent of your increase belongs to him. Whether it is given to Him or not, it still belongs to Him. To fail to give Him what is His is to rob God. Malachi 3:8 reads, "*Will a man rob or defraud God? Yet you rob and defraud Me. But ye say, Wherein have we robbed thee? [You have withheld your] tithes and offerings"* (Amplified).

Romans 2:22 reads, *"...do you rob temples [DO YOU APPROPRIATE TO YOUR OWN USE WHAT IS CONSECRATED TO GOD, thus robbing the sanctuary and doing sacrilege]?"* (Amplified). To fail to give God what is His is to dishonor Him. Tithing and giving offerings isn't a money issue — it is an honor issue!

Psalms 115:11-16, Amplified
11 You who [reverently] fear the Lord, trust in and lean on the Lord! He is their Help and their Shield.
12 The Lord has been mindful of us, He will bless us . . .
13 He will bless those who reverently and worshipfully fear the Lord, both small and great.
14 May the Lord give you increase more and more, YOU AND YOUR CHILDREN.
15 May you be blessed of the Lord, Who made heaven and earth!
16 The heavens are the Lord's heavens, but the earth has He given to the children of men.

When you honor and reverence the Lord, you benefit and your children benefit. But the flip side of that would also be true. If you fail to honor and reverence the Lord, you and your children will be affected. Failing to honor God opens the door to the devil; then, he can attack you. Failing to honor God with our finances is an open door to the enemy.

It is just best to give the honor to the Lord that is due Him, and one way you do that is by honoring Him with your tithes and offerings.

When you honor God, the Lord who made heaven and earth (verse 15) is the One who blesses you. If He can do such a great work as creating the heavens and the earth, can He not surely tend to your needs?

To those who honor Him, the outpoured blessing is so great that it cannot be contained in one generation. The blessing runs so deep that it reaches future generations yet unborn, for He will increase you and your children. Those who honor Him, He will honor (I Samuel 2:30).

CHAPTER 13

The Prosperous Soul

III John 1:2
Beloved, I wish above all things that thou mayest prosper and be in health, even as thy soul prospereth.

Although John wrote this letter, the Word tells us that men wrote the Bible as they were moved upon by the Holy Ghost. So, when the scripture reads, "*Beloved, I wish...*" (The word translated "wish" in the King James Version is "pray" in the original Greek.) this is really the desire of the Holy Spirit being expressed. The desire for your prosperity did not originate with you, but with God. He desires for your life to be prosperous. Your prosperity pleases God.

Psalms 35:27 reads, "*Let them shout for joy, and be glad, that favor my righteous cause: yea, let them say continually, Let the Lord be magnified, which HATH PLEASURE IN THE PROSPERITY OF HIS SERVANT.*" If God had pleasure in the prosperity of His servants, who were the Old Testament saints, how much greater would be His pleasure in the prosperity of His sons, those of us who are born again.

God desires your prosperity and has already provided for every need you will ever face.

When John wrote, "*Beloved, I wish above all things that thou mayest prosper and be in health, even as thy soul prospereth,*" you can see that your financial condition and the condition of your health are tied to the condition of your soul. (Your soul is made up of your mind, your will, and your emotions.)

The world links your prosperity with your job and your income, but God links your prosperity to the condition of your soul. Many believers will be diligent to tend to their job, but leave the condition of their soul woefully neglected.

Your prosperity is rooted in God, so that makes your prosperity as limitless as God Himself. Do not limit your prosperity to a paycheck. Your prosperity is rooted in God, so find out through his Word all that He has provided for you.

Tend to your soul by renewing your mind with the Word of God. Find out in the Word all that God has provided for you.

Prosperity does not pertain only to the financial arena, but to every arena of your life. God has provided for every arena of your life to prosper. Therefore, if any arena is suffering, dive into God's Word and see what God has to say about your situation.

If you fall behind financially, do not assume that it is strictly a financial problem. For the financial situation to be adjusted, many times there will have to be an adjustment in the soul first. You'll have to correct and adjust the way you're thinking and believing. Make your thinking come in line with God's Word.

Hosea 4:6 warns us, "*My people are destroyed for lack of knowledge....*" Before many financial problems in the lives of Christians can be dealt with, there is going to have to be an increase of the knowledge of the Word.

Many will spend countless hours pursuing more money, but they neglect their time in the Word. They do not grasp what John wrote, that their prosperity is connected to their soul, and the only thing that will bring about the prosperity of the soul is the Word. It is not more money they need; rather, they need more understanding and revelation that they are rich – they are made rich in Christ!

James 1:21 reads, "*... receive with meekness the engrafted word, which is able to save your souls.*" James was writing this to people who were born again. Although their spirits were saved, he was telling them that their souls still needed to be saved.

What did he mean by that? Remember that your soul is made up of your mind, your will, and your emotions. Although the life of God has been imparted into your spirit, your mind still needs to be saved or renewed. Now that you are born again, you need to allow the Word of God to direct your thinking.

James told them that they needed to receive the engrafted Word, and as they did, their souls would be saved. By feeding on the Word, you are feeding on God's thoughts. As you see through the Word what God's thoughts are, you are to take on His thoughts and His way of doing things. As you feed and act on the Word, it will become engrafted (rooted) in you, and it will save your soul.

Psalm 23:1-3 reads, "*The Lord is my shepherd; I shall not want. He maketh me to lie down in green pastures: he leadeth me beside still waters. HE RESTORETH MY SOUL....*" How does God restore your soul? Through His Word. As you feed on and act on His Word, your soul is restored, or saved, as James said. As you feed and act on God's Word, your mind is restored to right thinking; you begin to think like God thinks.

If Christians fail to feed and act on God's Word, He is unable to restore their souls, and their souls remain unsaved although they are born again and on their way to heaven. When Christians do not take the time to feed on the Word and restore their souls, or get their souls saved, then the devil can hold high carnival in their minds, and they live lives full of unnecessary hardship and crisis.

Paul tells us in Romans 12:2, "*And be not conformed to this world: but be ye transformed by the RENEWING OF YOUR MIND....*"

David called this process the "restoring of the soul". James called it the "saving of your soul". Paul called it the "renewing of your mind". They are all saying the same thing. The renewing of the mind is an ongoing process that you must do the rest of your life. If you ever stop feeding on the Word, your mind will slip back into its old way of thinking.

II Corinthians 10:4 & 5
4   (For the weapons of our warfare are not carnal, but mighty through God to the pulling down of STRONG HOLDS;)
5   Casting down IMAGINATIONS, and every high thing that exalteth itself against the knowledge of God, and bringing into captivity EVERY THOUGHT to the obedience of Christ;

We can see from this passage that Paul is telling us that these strong holds are in the mind; they are wrong thoughts and wrong ways of thinking. If you think wrong, you will believe wrong. Wrong thinking is the point of entrance for the enemy. If you think wrong, then you will talk wrong. If you talk wrong, then you open the door to the enemy. To walk in prosperity in every arena of life, you have to think right. Find out what God's Word says and bring your thinking in line with that.

In Ephesians 4:17 Paul warns us, "*...that you must no longer live as the heathen (Gentiles) do in their perverseness [in the folly, vanity and emptiness of their souls and the FUTILITY] OF THEIR MINDS*" (Amplified). Living out of the mind produces futile living. That is the way the unsaved live, but we are warned not to live life just being led by our minds, but we are to allow our spirits to dominate us.

The devil seeks to hold you in the mental arena, for that is his arena. He is the master of the mental arena. The devil can out-think you. But you are to hold him in the arena of faith, which is the spirit arena. Faith is in your spirit, not your mind.

If you try to believe God with your mind, you will not draw on faith, but you will draw on reason.

If you will allow your spirit to lead you, regardless of what your mind tells you, your faith will work for you.

When it comes to finances or any other arena, the devil fights to hold you in the mental arena, for then your faith will not work. If you are to live in God's supply, you must live beyond reasonings, and beyond what you can "figure out" and mentally calculate. Reason is doubt in disguise.

One reason Eve disobeyed God's Word is that she listened to what the serpent said. She carried on a conversation with him. The more she listened to the wrong thing, the more the wrong thing made sense to her. If you listen to the wrong thing long enough, it will start making sense to you. Just because it seems to make sense does not make it right. The question to ask yourself is, "Does it make Bible sense?"

Bring your thoughts in line with God's Word. When you are faced with a difficulty, ask yourself, "What does the Word say?" And think in line with what the Word says.

Remember, John told us that we would prosper and be in health to the same measure that our soul prospers. We will prosper to the same measure that we think right. The more we think in line with God's Word, the more we'll prosper. The less we think in line with God's Word, the less we'll prosper. Any unrenewed mind is a limited mind, but a renewed mind has the limitations removed.

God delights in the prosperity of His children, so talk about how abundant God's supply is for your life.

CHAPTER 14

Your Prosperity is Connected to Your Local Church

Psalm 92:13 & 14
13 Those that be PLANTED in the house of the Lord shall flourish in the courts of our God.
14 They shall still bring forth fruit in old age; they shall be fat and flourishing;

Your prosperity is connected to your local church. To flourish, you must bring your supply to the body of Christ by being planted in your local church.

Ephesians 4:16 tells us, "...*the whole body fitly joined together...which every joint supplieth....maketh increase of the body....*" God is the One who fits us together in the position in the body of Christ that pleases Him. The reason He puts us in that position is so we can bring our supply to the body of Christ. When we bring our supply, it causes increase in the body. However, if we are not functioning in the position God places us, we will not be bringing our supply to the body of Christ.

What does it mean to be fitly joined together? God knows where you fit in the body, so you must be in your place so you can bring a supply and also receive a supply. Prosperity is tied to your obedience to function where He assigns you, and to not let anything pull you away. Find out what local church God wants you in; then, stay planted there until He tells you otherwise.

Many are not flourishing in every arena of their lives because they have not planted themselves in a local church, and they are not bringing their supply to the body of Christ. God will lead you to the local church you are to be a part of, and you are to be a supply to that local church. You are to be a supply by:

1. Attending services

2. Giving tithes and offerings

3. Serving in the ministry of helps

4. Praying for your pastor and church family

When you do these things, not only will you cause that local body to increase, but you will personally increase. Remember, your prosperity is tied to your local church. If you want to flourish and be fat with the anointing of God, you have to stay planted in the place God puts you.

CHAPTER 15

Love in the Home

Years ago, I was focusing on teaching financial prosperity in our church when God spoke to me.

He said, "Financial prosperity is right and good to teach on, but you need to back up and teach the sheep about walking in love in their home. If they don't walk in love with each other in their home, they don't qualify for Bible prosperity."

Matthew 23:23 records that Jesus declared, "*Woe to you scribes and Pharisees, pretenders (hypocrites)! For you give a tenth of your mint and dill and cummin, and have neglected and omitted the weightier (more important) matters of the law – right and justice and mercy and fidelity. These you ought [particularly] to have done, without neglecting the others*" (Amplified). These religious leaders were certainly tithing, even down to the spices in their home, but they were not handling their relationships with people right.

Previous to this passage, Jesus had stated to them what the weightier matters were that must be obeyed in Matthew 22:37-40. "*Jesus said unto him, Thou shalt love the Lord thy God with all thy heart, and with all thy soul, and with all thy mind. This is the first and great commandment. And the second is like unto it, Thou shalt love thy neighbor as thyself. On these two commandments hang all the law and the prophets.*" What are the weightier matters that Jesus stated were to be done? Love toward God, and love toward other people.

All the tithing in the world will not take the place of failing to walk in love. You can tithe on everything that comes into your life, but if you do not walk in love, you won't have Bible prosperity. We are to do both – walk in love and tithe.

Our love walk must flourish in our home. Failing to walk in love with your spouse will keep you broke. Before you enter into a fight with your spouse or anyone else, ask yourself, "Do I have enough money to fund this strife?" The answer is, "No!"

Strife kills increase and causes you to lose what you do have.

Malachi 2:13-15, Amplified
13 "...the Lord does not regard your offering anymore or accept it with favor at your hand.
14 Yet you ask why does He reject it? Because the Lord was witness [to the covenant made at your marriage] between you and the wife of your youth, against whom you have dealt treacherously and to whom you were faithless. Yet she is your companion and the wife of your covenant [made by your marriage vows].
15 And did not God make [you and your wife] one [flesh]? Did not One make you and preserve your spirit alive? And why [did God make you two] one? Because He sought a godly offspring [from your union]. Therefore take heed to yourselves, and let no one deal treacherously and be faithless to the wife of his youth."

This passage shows us that the giving of tithes and offerings will never take the place of walking in love. This is what God was telling me when He told me that if Christians do not walk in love, they do not qualify for Bible prosperity. Not walking in love with one another will keep you broke, and all the extra work hours in the world will not be enough to fund the lack of love in home. Walking in love will put money in your pocket. It pays to walk in love. It causes you to qualify for Bible prosperity.

Be Generous to Your Own Family

Galatians 6:6 & 10, Amplified
6   Let him who receives instruction in the Word [of God] share all good things with his teacher [contributing to his support].
10 So then, as occasion and opportunity open up to us, let us do good... BE MINDFUL TO BE A BLESSING, especially to those of the household of faith...

We are told to be generous to those who impart the Word into our lives, but we are also instructed to be a blessing every time we have the opportunity, especially to those who are of the household of faith. Do you know that if your spouse and children are born again, they are of the household of faith?

If there was a minister you admired and were blessed by, you would show that by giving generously to them. Likewise, you should see the great blessing that your own spouse and children are to your own life, and you should be generous toward them. It's right to be generous toward other people, but if you are not generous toward your own family, you will never fully prosper.

Love will turn you into a giver! If a husband would put his wife first, seeing to it that her desires are met, and the wife would put the husband first, seeing to it that his desires are met, there would be heaven in the home. If it is important to your spouse, make it important to you.

To qualify for Bible prosperity, you have to walk in love in your home, and love will cause you to be generous toward those in your own household. Love is a giver!

CHAPTER 16

Bless What You Have

Mark 6:35-44

35 And when the day was now far spent, his disciples came unto him, and said, This is a desert place, and now the time is far passed:

36 Send them away, that they may go into the country round about, and into the villages, and buy themselves bread: for they have nothing to eat.

37 He answered and said unto them, Give ye them to eat. And they say unto him, Shall we go and buy two hundred pennyworth of bread, and give them to eat?

38 He saith unto them, How many loaves have ye? go and see. And when they knew, they say, Five, and two fishes.

39 And he commanded them to make all sit down by companies upon the green grass.

40 And they sat down in ranks, by hundreds, and by fifties.

41 And when he had taken the five loaves and two fishes, HE LOOKED UP TO HEAVEN AND BLESSED, and brake the loaves, and gave them to his disciples to set before them; and the two fishes divided he among them all.

42 And they did all eat, and were filled.

43 And they took up twelve baskets full of the fragments, and of the fishes.

44 And they that did eat of the loaves were about five thousand men.

There were times during Jesus' earthly ministry that He was faced with not having enough. What did He do? This passage of scripture shows us.

Jesus has His disciples to bring Him something He can use – a little boy's lunch, five loaves and two fish. No, this is not enough for the multitude as it is, but once faith is attached to it, it will not stay as it is. Faith will not leave it as it found it.

Jesus instructs the disciples to have the multitude of approximately 20,000 people to be organized. They sat them down in companies of fifty.

Many Christians fail to realize the significance of this step when exercising faith for supply. Organization played a role in setting the stage to receive multiplication. If God were to multiply the food without there being proper order, there would have been multiplied chaos. Proper order is imperative to receive a greater supply, for God is a God of order.

If you need God to bring increase to an arena of your life, then get that arena organized so that it can receive multiplication.

After the disciples had brought order to the multitude, Jesus took the loaves and fish in His hands and looked up to heaven. When you are faced with need, and when you are exercising faith, it matters which direction you look. It matters what holds your attention.

Jesus looked up to heaven and blessed the loaves and fish. He did not complain about what He did not have, but He blessed what He did have. He did not wait for God to bless it. He blessed it. He blessed it while it was still in its un-multiplied form. When it was not enough, He blessed it – He did not curse it. He did not curse what He had that was not enough by complaining, griping, murmuring or worrying about it. Rather, He blessed it!

When you do not have enough, do not curse it by complaining, griping or worrying – bless it! Thank God for what you do have. You have to show gratitude for what you do have if you are going to receive more.

An ungrateful heart is a poor receiver and cannot receive more. It is not that God withholds, but lack of gratitude cannot receive.

Lack of gratitude is an open door to the enemy to rob you of blessings God wants you to have. Lack of gratitude shuts down faith and keeps it from working. If you want a better home, do not criticize or complain about the one you do have. The one you have may not be the one you want, but you are to be thankful for what you do have; then, your faith will work when you believe God for the one you do want. Show gratitude for what you do have by being thankful. Then your faith will work when you do say, "Thank you, Father, for what I do have, but I am reaching for more with my faith to lay hold of the home I desire."

If you need a new car, a new job, or whatever your need may be, the same principle is true. Be thankful for what you have, organize it, bless what you do have with your words, and then release your faith for more.

James 3:10 warns us, "*Out of the same mouth proceedeth blessing and cursing. My brethren, these things ought not so to be.*" The cursing spoken of here is not referring to speaking words of profanity, but speaking anything that is not of faith. Complaining, criticizing and griping are void of faith, and full of doubt and unbelief. "*...Whatsoever is not of faith is sin*" (Romans 14:23).

That which blesses is to flow from our mouth, not what curses.

When God delivered His people from slavery in Egypt, He endeavored to lead them to the land He had given them, but because of their unbelief, they complained and murmured against God and Moses. When they did, they suffered great tragedy.

Serpents bit them and multitudes died; fire fell in their camp and consumed them, and they were left to wander in the wilderness until that whole generation died off.

Complaining, criticizing and murmuring will never lead you to your desired place. It will leave you wandering in the wilderness, never arriving.

God has given us the spirit of faith (Second Corinthians 4:13). So let us speak faith words, and words of gratitude. Faith words will carry us into multiplication.

Deuteronomy 28:47 & 48, Amplified
47 Because you did not serve the Lord your God with JOY-FULNESS of [mind and] heart [in gratitude] for the abundance of all [with which He had blessed you],
48 Therefore, you shall serve your enemies...

It is a joy to serve God, and that joy is a weapon that protects you from the enemy. Joy is a decision and not a feeling.

Decide to be grateful, thankful and joyful, and do all that He has assigned to your life with joy and gratitude. Then your faith will work for you when you need to receive from God.

When Jesus blessed what He had, it became more than enough. Look up to heaven and bless what you have, and it will become more than enough!

CHAPTER 17

Mix Faith with the Word

Hebrews 4:2
"...the word preached did not profit them, not being mixed with faith in them that heard it."

Is it possible to hear the Word of God and not profit from it? Absolutely! The Word must be mixed with faith, and when it is, there will be undeniable profit and increase.

Just as a chemist in a laboratory will not get any reaction until he mixes certain elements together, there will be no reaction of the Word until faith is mixed with it.

How do you mix faith with the Word? The tongue is the mixer that combines faith with the Word. When your words of faith are mixed with God's Word, you are going to get a divine reaction.

Luke 1:26, 27, 30, 31, & 38
26 And in the sixth month the angel Gabriel was sent from God into a city of Galilee, named Nazareth,
27 To a virgin espoused to a man whose name was Joseph, of the house of David; and the virgin's name was Mary.
30 And the angel said unto her, Fear not, Mary: for thou hast found favour with God.
31 And behold, thou shalt conceive in thy womb, and bring forth a son, and shalt call his name Jesus.
38 And Mary said, Behold the handmaid of the Lord; BE IT UNTO ME ACCORDING TO THY WORD..."

When Mary responded to the angel with words that agreed with God's will, then God's will and God's Word could come to pass. Mary was mixing faith with God's will and God's Word by agreeing with God's Word.

When you speak words of faith that agree with God's Word, then you are mixing faith with God's Word and you will profit from it. Notice that God had a plan for Mary, but Mary had to agree with that plan before He could bring it to pass.

God has a health plan and a financial plan for you, but you have to speak words of faith that agree with His plan before He can bring it to pass. It is not enough that God wants to do something in your life. You have to agree with it before He can do it. Your verbal agreement starts the process. God has provided a supply for you, but you must speak words that agree with God's Word if you are to receive that supply. If you speak against your supply, you will keep it from reaching you.

If you talk about the lack of money, it will keep it from coming in. Rather, talk about how your Heavenly Father is supplying every need in your life. Speak words of faith that agree with God's supply in your life, and then it can reach you.

Be a Doer of the Word

Luke 11:27 & 28, KJV
27 And it came to pass, as he spake these things, a certain woman of the company lifted up her voice, and said unto him, Blessed is the womb that bare thee...
28 But he said, Yea rather, blessed are they that HEAR the word of God, and KEEP IT.

Luke 11:28, Amplified
28 But He said Blessed...rather are those who HEAR the Word of God and OBEY and PRACTICE it!

In this passage, we see a woman magnifying Mary because she

gave birth to Jesus. But Jesus corrected her. He said that the person that's blessed is the one who hears the Word and does it. He's saying that those who hear and do the Word are more blessed than the woman who gave birth to Him. The doing of the Word exalts a person into a place of blessing.

Be a doer of the Word in your actions, but another way of being a doer of the Word is by speaking words in line with God's Word.

Your faith cannot be heard until you speak. Your spirit cannot be heard until you speak. Make your mouth do its work!

Are You IN the Faith?

II Corinthians 13:5
Examine yourselves, whether ye be IN the faith...

Did you know that you could have faith and still not be in faith?

Just because I have a car doesn't mean I'm in the car. Just because I have a house doesn't mean that I'm in the house.

Likewise, just because you have faith does not mean that you are in faith. Make sure that you are in faith. How do you do that? Through the words you speak and through your actions.

II Corinthians 13:5, Amplified
Examine and test and evaluate your own selves to see whether you are HOLDING TO YOUR FAITH and showing the proper fruits of it. Test and prove yourselves [not Christ].

Since my dad is a cotton and wheat farmer, he knows how important it is to inspect his crops to see how they're doing. Every day he evaluates the condition of every crop. He knows that in a short time something can happen that could affect his harvest, so he is very watchful over the crops. He makes sure that each field is producing.

Likewise, you should watch over every arena of your life to make sure that each arena is producing the right harvest. If you see an area lagging behind, you need to increase the amount of faith you're exercising in that area. If you fail to pay attention to just one arena of your life, that's the arena the enemy can gain access through.

You are to examine your faith walk; not so you can accuse yourself of failure, but so you can see what you need to fortify. If you are exercising faith in an arena, but seeing no results, then you need to make changes.

When you are correctly exercising faith in the Word of God, you're going to get results; things are going to change. But if you've been endeavoring to believe God over a long period of time, and there's no improvement, see what changes you need to make on your end.

When Christians have been endeavoring to believe God over a period of time for a change in a situation, but getting no results, many times it's because they're trying to believe God with their mind. When endeavoring to believe God with the mind, it fails every time. But when believing God with the heart, it works every time.

Faith is of the heart, not the mind. The mind cannot conduct faith, only the heart can conduct faith. If you try to believe God with the mind, you will slip into reasonings and questions. But faith is in the heart of the believer. Faith just rests on what God says and refuses to try to reason out or figure out the answer mentally.

When making a road trip across country in a car, you check the map frequently to see if you are on the right road. Likewise, check up on yourself to see if you are on the right road concerning your faith. Don't just end up in a place you didn't intend to go to, and then wonder how you got there.

As Second Corinthians 13:5 says, evaluate yourself to see if you are, "...*holding to your faith and showing the proper fruits of it. Test and prove yourselves [not Christ].*" When you are holding to faith, there will be proper fruits of it. If there is not proper fruit, then check up to see what you are holding to.

If you get disturbed and troubled if there is a change in your job, then it shows that you are holding to the job instead of holding to God's Word. Do not attach your faith to your job. Attach your faith to God's Word, and it will support you no matter what changes go on around you.

When your faith is in God, then you're looking to Him as your Provider and not to your job. Your job is simply an avenue through which God will bless you, but it is not your provider – God is.

"...*Test and prove yourselves [not Christ].*" In other words, it's your faith that's on trial, not Christ. If there is failure in your life somewhere, it's a faith failure, and not God failing you.

Fortify your faith, feed your faith through God's Word, then speak and act on your faith, and change any failure into victory.

The Call of Faith

In Romans 4:17 we see the definition of faith. Faith "...*CALLETH those things which be not as though they were.*" Faith's job is to call it as you want it and not as it is.

If you do not have enough money to meet your financial obligations, call yourself fully supplied. If you do not have a job, call for the right job to come to you. Faith has a call.

If you talk about your lack of money, you will keep it from coming in. If you talk about your lack of business, then that is what you'll have. But that's not how faith talks. Faith calls what you want to come to you. Call in your supply, call in the job you need, call in the customers to your business.

It's the job of faith to call – not to "figure it out". It's not your job to mentally calculate and wonder when it's going to come and wonder how God is going to do it. That is all reasonings, and reason is doubt in disguise. That is all the mental arena. Get out of the mental arena and hook your mouth up to your spirit and call. Your answer is waiting on your call!

Loose Your Supply

All through Jesus' earthly ministry, we see Him using His words to draw His supply to Him. At different times of need in His ministry, His supply did not come to Him automatically; He had to exercise faith.

On one occasion, He needed a colt, so He told His disciples where to find it and the words to say to the owner. When the disciples found the colt, it was tied up, but when they said to the owner what Jesus told them, the colt was released, and Jesus' supply came to Him.

Sometimes, your supply may be tied up somewhere else, but your words of faith and your call of faith will loose your supply and cause it to come to you.

Jesus told us in the last phrase of Mark 11:23, "*...he shall have whatsoever he saith*." The more you say it, the more you will have it. The less you say it, the less you will have it. So, stay with it. Make your mouth do its work!

Faith that Takes

Mark 11:24
Therefore, I say unto you, what things so ever ye desire, when ye pray, believe that ye receive them, and ye shall have them.

The Greek (The New Testament was originally written in Greek) actually reads, "*...What things so ever ye desire, when ye pray, believe that ye TAKE them, and ye shall have them.*" The things that you desire are yours for the taking. It pleases God when you lay hold of what He has provided for your life and make them yours.

We can see from Mark 11:24 that God *authorizes* you to believe that the answer is yours at the time you pray.

I John 5:14 & 15
14 ...if we ask anything according to his will (Word)**, he heareth us:**
15 And if we know that he hear us...we know that we have...

Since we can know that we have it, we take it as our own.

At the time we pray, God hears us. At the time we pray, He sends the answer right then. He authorizes us to consider the answer ours, simply because He sent the answer at the time we prayed, even though it might not have manifested yet.

From the time He sent it until the time it manifests, we are to rejoice because the answer is ours, and we are confident that it shall manifest because He sent it when we asked.

Until it does manifest, we are to continue rejoicing as we stand our ground against any thought that suggests otherwise. No matter what thoughts of doubt may try to come, we stand our ground against them, keeping the switch of faith turned on because we know that God already sent our answer. It's easy to rejoice when the answer manifests, but faith rejoices even before the answer shows up because it knows God sent it.

Standing on the Word in faith is a part of the Word just as much as receiving is part of the Word. Anyone will rejoice when the answer appears, but true faith rejoices *before* it appears.

Even after you receive your answer from God, you still must exercise faith to maintain what you have received. The enemy is busy trying to take from us all that God has blessed us with, but we not only stand our ground until our answer appears, but even after it appears, we uphold our answer with our faith.

Even after creating the universe, God continues to maintain it, for Hebrews 1:3 tells us that He is, "...*upholding all things by the word of his power.*" No matter what you receive from God, you will have to continue to maintain it by continuing to speak words of faith. It is not enough to receive it; you must maintain it.

Words of faith hold God's blessings in your life. Continue to speak words of faith, for the just shall live by faith.

CHAPTER 18

Put Spiritual Things First

Matthew 6:33
But seek ye FIRST the kingdom of God, and his righteousness; and all these things (daily necessities) **shall be ADDED unto you.**

God's kingdom is a spiritual kingdom. We are to put spiritual things first, and when we do, we can be assured that God will add to us.

To put spiritual things first is to make the education and the development of your spirit a priority. You educate and develop your own spirit through feeding on God's Word and fellowshipping with Him in prayer.

To put spiritual things first is to make what's important to God, important to you. The body of Christ is important to God. Bringing your supply to the body of Christ must become a priority to you.

The best way to bring your supply to the body of Christ is to be planted in the local church God leads you to and be faithful to serve there. Being faithful to your local church involves:

1. Attending services

2. Giving tithes and offerings

3. Serving in the ministry of helps

4. Praying for the pastor and the congregation

To put natural things first will hinder the flow of God's supply in your life. To put the pursuit of money before spiritual things will lead to poverty of the worst kind – spiritual poverty; then, nothing works as it should.

God's plan is that as you put spiritual things first; then, He can add to you.

Deuteronomy 28:1 & 2
1   And it shall come to pass, if thou shalt hearken diligently unto the voice of the Lord thy God, to observe and do all his commandments which I command thee this day, that the Lord thy God will set thee on high above all nations of the earth:
2   And all these blessings shall COME ON THEE, and OVER-TAKE thee, if thou shalt hearken unto the voice of the Lord thy God.

In running a race, if another runner runs alongside you, keeping pace with you, he has come on you. If the runner passes you and gets out in from of you, he precedes you and overtakes you.

Likewise, God said that if we are doers of His Word, His blessings will come on us, which means that they will keep pace with us. But they will not only come on us, they will also overtake us. They will precede us, going in front of us and prepare the way for us.

This all belongs to the doer of the Word, one who puts God's Word first in his life.

CHAPTER 19

Willing and Obedient

Isaiah 1:19
If ye be willing and obedient, ye shall eat the good of the land:

Willingness and obedience to fulfill God's plan is key to your prosperity. Willingness is bringing your own will into harmony with God's will for your life; it is the agreement with God's plan in your spirit. Obedience is the actual walking out of that plan. If you are to prosper, both must be in place in your life – willingness and obedience.

Many people struggle because they have not been obedient to God's plan, but it always pays to agree with God's plan for your life and to obey it. To fail to obey is to give place to the devil.

Years ago, when we started our church in California, I conducted all the services while my husband continued traveling full-time in the ministry. Although I was conducting all the services, I still did not agree on the inside of me that I was the pastor. My husband told me I was, but I didn't believe him. I didn't want to be the pastor because I liked traveling.

Several years later, God dealt with me that I was the pastor. When He did, I made the adjustment in my spirit, agreeing with His plan for me to be pastor. Up until that time, I had been obedient, but I had not been willing in my spirit. When I finally became willing, we started increasing.

Those called to the fivefold ministry must be willing to occupy the office God has called them to instead of forming their own plan and trying to occupy an office God didn't call them to. To try to occupy a place God never called you to will result in struggle and dissatisfaction. Nothing will work for you as it should until you become willing and obedient to God's plan.

God's plan for your life carries peace, health, fulfillment and fullness of supply. Live in God's plan and live in God's supply.

CHAPTER 20

A Life of Faith

Philippians 4:11-13, Amplified
11 Not that I was implying that I was in any personal want, for I have learned how to be content (satisfied to the point where I am not disturbed or disquieted) in whatever state I am.
12 I know how to be abased and live humbly in straightened circumstances, and I know also how to enjoy plenty and live in abundance. I have learned in any and all circumstances the secret of facing every situation, whether well-fed or going hungry, having a sufficiency and enough to spare or going without and being in want.
13 I have strength for all things in Christ Who empowers me [I am ready for anything and equal to anything through Him who infuses inner strength into me; I am self-sufficient in Christ's sufficiency].

Real faith means that you have learned how to live utterly independent of circumstances.

There may be times when you have more finances than you do at other times. Paul even experienced this for he stated, "*I know how to be abased and live humbly in straightened circumstances, and I know how to enjoy plenty and live in abundance.*"

Someone may say, "I know how to live in abundance. It's easy to live when there's an abundance of money!"

Many don't know how to live in abundance. When there's an abundance of money, they backslide from God, neglect church services, and quit exercising their faith, for they begin trusting in money and not in God. They don't know how to live in abundance.

Still someone else may say, "I know, like Paul, how to live humbly and in straightened circumstances. I've been living that way for most of my life!"

Paul didn't live in straightened circumstances all the time. He knew how to exercise faith and receive the supply he needed.

Paul knew how to live when there was little money, and he knew how to live when there was a lot of money – he lived by faith!

If you don't live by faith when there's just a little bit of money, you will stay there in that place of need. If you don't live by faith when there is more than enough money, then you will start trusting in money instead of God, then you could lose what you do have.

Living by faith is the only way to live. It will cause you to stay the same, even when circumstances change.

A Doer of the Word

Matthew 7:24-27
24 Therefore whosoever heareth these sayings of mine, and doeth them, I will liken him unto a wise man, which built his house upon a rock:
25 And the rain descended, and the floods came, and the winds blew, and beat upon that house; and it fell not: for it was founded upon a rock.
26 And everyone that heareth these sayings of mine, and doeth them not, shall be likened unto a foolish man, which built his house upon the sand:
27 And the rain descended, and the floods came, and the winds blew, and beat upon that house; and it fell: and great was the fall of it.

In this passage of scripture, the house is really a man's life.

The storms of life are going to come to every man, and it's the doer of the Word who will be left standing. The man who was prepared for the storm was the one who was a doer of the Word on the sunny days, when there was no storm in view; then, he kept being a doer of the Word in the face of the storm. The house that didn't fall was built on the right thing prior to the storm. It matters what you are building on prior to the storm. But if you find yourself unprepared for a storm you may be facing, begin now feeding on the Word and being a doer of it. It is your answer.

Just because you can feel the storm doesn't mean you're failing and that your faith isn't working. Your mind and your body are going to feel the storm. The house is going to feel the storm, but that doesn't mean the house will collapse. No matter what you're feeling, keep standing your ground on God's Word, and when the storm passes, you'll still be standing.

The storm has no mercy on the one who loves God. It's not enough to love God in the face of the storm – you have to be a doer of the Word.

Remember this, storms will come, but the doer of the Word determines the outcome.

CHAPTER 21

Faithful in Business

Romans 12:11
Not slothful in business...

Some Christians stay in a place of financial need because of the way they conduct their business affairs.

If you're slothful in your business affairs, you won't prosper the way God wants you to. If you're unorganized, unreliable or produce a poor quality of work, you won't prosper fully. If you don't keep your word in business affairs, if you're late to your appointments, speak negatively about your boss or fellow co-workers, if you're dishonest in your financial dealings, you won't prosper as God wants you to.

During the early days of the church, there were multitudes being added to the church, and the business needs of the church increased drastically. The apostles told the congregation, "...*look ye out among you seven men of honest report, full of the Holy Ghost and wisdom, whom we may appoint over this business*" (Acts 6:3). These men that were appointed weren't ministers; these were businessmen.

The criteria the Holy Ghost laid out for these businessmen was that they had to be:

1) Men of honest report. You sure wouldn't want someone handling the business and finances if they weren't honest.

2) Full of the Holy Ghost. They were to be spiritual men.

3) Full of wisdom

These characteristics are recognizable in a person, or the congregation wouldn't have been able to choose them.

Just as financial poverty will hold a person back from accomplishing all they have in their heart, a poverty of excellence will hold back a person from accomplishing all that is in their heart.

If you want to live in Bible prosperity, there has to be a spirit of excellence in all you do.

God wants to bless us, but He can only bless us as we are doers of the Word in every area of life – even in the business arena.

CHAPTER 22

Bought with a Price

I Corinthians 6:19 & 20
**19 What? Know ye not that your body is the temple of the
Holy Ghost which is in you, which ye have of God, and YE ARE
NOT YOUR OWN?**
**20 FOR YE ARE BOUGHT WITH A PRICE: therefore glorify God
in your body, and in your spirit, WHICH ARE GOD'S.**

We belong to God, for we were purchased by the blood of
Jesus.

He bought you, and you received His loving Lordship when you
called on the name of the Lord for your salvation. As the scripture
above states, your body and your spirit are God's – you belong to
Him.

Since we belong to Him, all that we have is His. We do not own
ourselves, and nothing we possess is ours; it's His.

We are not owners; we are stewards. All that's in our possession He has made us stewards of.

A steward does not have ownership; he simply manages his
master's possessions. When the master gives the steward an
instruction, a steward promptly carries out those instructions, for
he realizes that which is in his possession belongs to the master.
The master is the owner, not him.

When we understand this, we cease to struggle with instructions our Father gives us. When He instructs us to give tithes and

offerings, or anything else, as stewards, we are to simply obey. We are carrying out the instructions of the owner.

The beauty of our wonderful Lord and Master is that when we obey the Master's instructions, He blesses, rewards and increases us for giving Him what was His all along.

He is not a hard task master to be feared; but rather, He is a loving Lord who has made us partakers of His divine nature and sharers of the inheritance in Christ. We are His, and He has made Himself responsible to supply and provide for us in every arena of life. He loves to provide for us.

CHAPTER 23

Steps to Receiving Your Supply

If you're facing financial difficulties, there are steps you can take to receive your supply.

1) Make a detailed list of your financial needs. List any items that need to be paid off, and any items you need to purchase.

2) Make a list of scriptures that show you the supply that is yours in Christ, and spend time meditating on those scriptures.

3) In prayer, call out those needs before God, and claim the supply that is yours.

  a) Claim the amount of money you need.

  b) Tell Satan to take his hand off the supply that is yours.

  c) Loose the ministering spirits, the angels, to go and cause the money to come into your hands.

4) Take time *daily* to thank God for the supply that is coming into your hands. Thank Him for the supply for each thing you need. Using the list of scriptures that you made, confess them over your situation, thanking God for His Word that's working in your behalf.

Refuse to Worry

If your faith is to work, you must cast the care of your situation over on the Lord and refuse to worry.

Philippians 4:6 & 7, Amplified
6   Do not fret or have any anxiety about anything, but in every circumstance and in everything, by prayer and petition (definite requests), with thanksgiving, continue to make your wants known to God.
7   And God's peace [shall be yours...

I Peter 5:7, Amplified
Casting the whole of your care [all of your anxieties, all your worries, all your concerns, once and for all] on Him, for He cares for you affectionately and cares about you watchfully.

If the temptation to worry comes to you, refuse it. Remind yourself that because you have cast your care on Him, He is taking care of your situation, and then don't touch it in your thought life. If you're going to worry about your situation, He can't take care of it because you have it. But if you will cast it on Him, and leave it with Him, then He will be able to take care of it.

How do you know if you're worrying about it? If you're thinking about it.

If your faith is going to work, you must refuse to worry, and you must guard your thought life. Be a doer of the Word. Cast your care on Him, trusting that He will work in your behalf as you hold fast to confessing His Word and thanking Him for it.

Greater is He that's in you than He that's in the world. Believe that. Confess that the Greater One is working in your behalf.

God has provided an abundant supply for all of His children, and the hand of faith is what lays hold of that supply and brings it into your life. No matter what need you may face in life, God has provided the supply, and it's yours for the taking!

Reach out for all He has provided for you, and in the face of every circumstance, bodly declare, "I have a supply!"

A Sinner's Prayer To Receive Jesus As Savior

Dear Heavenly Father:

I come to You in the Name of Jesus. Your Word says, "...*him that cometh to me I will in no wise cast out*" (John 6:37).

So I know You won't cast me out; but You will take me in, and I thank You for it.

You said in Your Word, "...*If thou shalt confess with thy mouth the Lord Jesus, and shall believe in thine heart that God has raised him from the deat, thou shalt be saved...For whosoever shall call upon the name of the Lord shall be saved*" (Romans 10:9, 13).

I believe in my heart that Jesus Christ is the Son of God. I believe Jesus died for my sins and was raised from the dead so I could be in right – standing with God. I am calling upon His Name, the Name of Jesus, so I know, Father, that You save me now.

Your Word says, "...*with the heart man believeth unto right-eousness; and with the mouth confession is made unto salvation*" (Romans 10:10). I do believe with my heart, and I confess Jesus now as my Lord. Therefore, I am saved! Thank You, Father.